PERFECTLY SIMPLE ICE CREAM

Perfectly Simple
ice cream

100 RECIPES *anyone* CANMAKE

ANTHONY
TASSINELLO

MARY JO
THORESEN

foreword by
Alice Waters

PHOTOGRAPHY BY **KELLY ISHIKAWA**
STYLING BY **ROD HIPSKIND**

**callisto
publishing**
an imprint of Sourcebooks

To Curt. And to Mom and Dad.
—MARY JO

Originally published as *Ice Cream Social* in 2016 in the United States of America by Rockridge Press, an imprint of Callisto Publishing. This edition issued based on the paperback edition published in 2016 in the United States of America by Rockridge Press, an imprint of Callisto Publishing.

Published by Callisto Publishing LLC C/O Sourcebooks LLC
P.O. Box 4410, Naperville, Illinois 60567-4410
(630) 961-3900
callistopublishing.com

Printed and bound in the United States of America.
VP 10 9 8 7 6 5 4 3 2 1

CONTENTS

FOREWORD

A T CHEZ PANISSE, we always have ice cream on the menu. Perfectly scooped and served on its own or paired with a perfect slice of tart, ice cream has a kind of universal appeal. When made simply, using fresh, local, organic ingredients, ice cream can evoke the feelings of a season or the treasured memory of a childhood delight.

Everyone who eats at Chez Panisse looks forward to the mulberry ice cream or Howard's miracle plum sherbet in the summer. In the winter months, when the weather changes and fresh fruit comes in limited supply, our menu changes, too. Fruit syrups can be prepared and preserved for later, and we never go without an ample supply of chocolate, toasted nuts, and candied citrus on hand.

Pastry chefs Anthony Tassinello and Mary Jo Thoresen have decades of experience creating and thinking about the desserts we serve at the restaurant. Everything in this book has their expansive and exhaustive knowledge behind it.

As a part of our Chez Panisse family, Anthony and Mary Jo are also an expression of the important principles we practice—honoring the farmers, thinking with the seasons, and cooking with equal measures of freedom and restraint.

ALICE WATERS
Owner, Chez Panisse Restaurant
Founder, Edible Schoolyard Project

INTRODUCTION

WHO DOESN'T LOVE ice cream? We remember the excitement of going to the local dairy on a hot summer evening in search of cool relief. A scoop of sweet, creamy ice cream mounded atop a sugar cone was our siren song. Who among us, when hearing the jingle of the approaching ice cream truck, did not feel their pulse quicken? Children lined up anxiously, money in hand, while the ice cream man, like a magician in white, unveiled treats for all who managed to track him down.

Each and every time, the ritual of ice cream is a special treat. However it is served, be it in a cone, float, shake, sandwich, sundae, or simply a solitary scoop, ice cream seems to go with just about every occasion.

The history of ice cream likely begins with China's emperors, who would send slaves to the mountains with the task of bringing back ice and snow, which were then transformed into a frozen confection made with milk, flour, and camphor. Popular flavors for the time included honey, pomegranate, and quince.

"Iced" creams have been made for centuries by taking heavy cream or custard, flavoring it with fruit, and then chilling the mixture in pewter or tin pots submerged in ice and salt. Through experimentation, the freezing technique was gradually refined. The method of stirring the mixture during the freezing process to prevent ice crystals from forming was a great improvement and yielded a smoother, creamier texture. No longer a closely guarded secret, and originally enjoyed solely by royalty and the well-off, ice cream was now available to everyone. We could not be more pleased for this delicious progress!

Over the past decade, artisanal ice cream shops have popped up all over the country. People are seeking out handmade ice creams over mass-produced, commercially made products. One bite is all that is needed to reinforce your decision; the quality of a handmade artisanal ice cream wins every time. And in the end, ice cream is a relatively simple thing to make. It essentially requires four ingredients for a base; by adding in an almost infinite choice of flavorings and fold-ins, you create a simple, delicious dessert.

Summer and ice cream are a natural combination. Is it any wonder, then, that July is National Ice Cream month? And the third Sunday in July is National Ice Cream Day.

Make the worthwhile investment of an ice cream maker of the highest quality that your budget will allow. Even if you use the finest ingredients available, a poor-quality machine will not yield the texture and smoothness a superior machine can provide. It is easy to do a little research and find just the right partner for your ice cream adventures, as most kitchen stores now offer several machines in various price ranges, all designed for home use.

Our goal here is not only to tempt—that goes without saying—but also to prepare you to embrace the process of creating your own ice cream, sherbets, frozen yogurts, and granitas. The starting point begins with the basic knowledge and recipes we offer here. Master these easy methods, then begin to curate your own library of flavors! Keep in mind: A recipe is merely a guideline. Ultimately, we encourage you to determine how to flavor your final mixture—you are the artisan. Let your palate be your guide; trust it, and you will graduate from recipe follower to ice cream creator. It's a wide world of frozen desserts out there, so think outside the carton. Add, subtract, or substitute flavoring ingredients based on what you have available. Perhaps

there is a particularly aromatic cinnamon in your spice drawer when a recipe calls for nutmeg? Or a cache of nuts that you need to use? Nuts can be swapped freely in and out of recipes. No brandy on hand for your creation? Reach for the bourbon instead. Be adventurous and embrace what your ice cream sensibilities tell you.

We predict that you will love making your own frozen treats so much that you will be planning your own ice cream social before very long. What a fantastic way to meet the new (or old) neighbors, entertain friends, or simply fulfill a craving.

Follow us to the freezer!

ingredients and equipment

The wonderful thing about making ice creams, sherbets, granitas, and the other recipes in this book is their simplicity. Whether you are new to the craft of making your own ice cream or looking for fresh ideas, you'll find that frozen treats are surprisingly easy to experiment with in your own kitchen. Common ingredients are combined, then transformed by using time-tested techniques that will have you churning out winning combinations—and quite possibly a few undiscovered concoctions of your own—in short order.

As you prepare for the rewarding endeavor of creating delicious frozen desserts at home, let's first review the basic ingredients and equipment that you will be turning to again and again on your ice cream journey. These are the secrets to amazing homemade ice cream.

THE INGREDIENTS

When we first started discussing the idea of writing an ice cream book, we wanted to share with ice cream enthusiasts not only the years of professional experience we have, but also the fun and passion we have for what is arguably the world's favorite dessert. Our conversations ranged from tales of travel to work experiences and the people that influenced our training through the years. Eventually we would come full circle, with one recurring message: Seek out the finest ingredients available, then stay out of their way.

What we mean by this is that there is an advantage in *not* doing too much to ingredients. When you find yourself with prime components, use them so they are elevated by a sprinkle of sugar or a splash of liqueur. Often, just a little goes a long way. Complement existing flavors with fine chocolate or perfectly ripe fruit; you will be developing skills that will be refined over time. Keep track of your particular triumphs or pitfalls—from the broadest down to the teaspoon—knowing that the perfect mixture is in there somewhere! It is interesting

The ice cream cone made its debut in 1904 at the St. Louis World's Fair.

to look back on your learning process and remember how delicious or oddball a particular combination wound up.

Our recipes are intended to appeal to all levels of cooking experience, but with a particular nod toward the beginner. This allows much of your attention to be focused on procuring the ripest fruits, freshest nuts, most exotic aromatic spices, and finest chocolates that you can afford. Educating yourself about quality components and what to look for when shopping is nearly as important as the techniques you will add to your repertoire. The streamlined recipes we provide ensure that these precious ingredients are put to good use and, ultimately, that the result is a delicious finished dessert.

Delightfully simple and satisfying frozen treats can be made with a handful of easily attainable ingredients: whole milk or half-and-half, heavy (whipping) cream, eggs, sugar, and salt.

ORGANIC First, a few words on the importance of using organic ingredients. Your ice cream will only be as good as your ingredients, and choosing organic will give you a better tasting dessert. You will also be supporting a network dedicated to bringing us wholesome food, people who are renewing the soil with farming practices that are sustainable and natural. Support organic farmers and choose these fruits for your recipes. It can be such a pleasure to shop the local farmers' market and meet the farmers, taste the produce, and learn about varietals. Many grocery stores around the country also offer an impressive selection of organic produce. Choose milk and cream from organic sources. Seek out eggs from hens that are fed organic feed and allowed to run around and be chickens. Lucky for all of us, organic produce, eggs, milk, cream, and butter are widely available these days, a testament to the power of these values.

DAIRY The backbone of any great ice cream is the quality of the dairy products you select. By choosing organic milk and cream, you are already on a path to a delicious finished treat. Additionally, they will be free from any growth hormones and antibiotics. While these products cost a bit more, the resulting flavor of your frozen treats will justify the added expense.

EGGS The richness of your ice cream custard base is derived from protein-rich egg yolks. A rich egg custard is a harmonious blend of milk, cream, and sugar thickened slowly over gentle heat. Choose extra large organic eggs, which are the standard size for all the recipes in this book.

SUGAR By "sugar" we mean organic granulated sugar, unless otherwise noted in recipes where confectioners sugar is called for. Organic sugar and confectioners sugar are widely available at better grocers and online.

SALT When we call for salt, we mean ordinary kosher salt, though we do also love the haunting, otherworldly crunch of *fleur de sel;* using it as a garnish adds a funky, fun dimension to frozen desserts.

CHOCOLATE Volumes have been written about chocolate and its cultural and culinary significance, so of course we dedicate an entire chapter of recipes to this marvelous ingredient. We love the dark, bittersweet offerings from artisanal makers such as TCHO or Guittard in the San Francisco Bay Area, Amano Chocolate in Orem, Utah, Valrhona, and Green & Black's. Whichever brand you use, a minimum of 60 percent cacao will ensure an honest chocolate note in your finished ice cream. For bolder results, explore the spectrum of higher cacao percentages.

FRUIT Choosing fruit that is organic and in season makes sense in every way. Fruit is at its peak, its most plentiful and most affordable. It will be free of sprays and pesticides that do not belong in our soil or in our bodies. Again, shopping your local farmers' market as often as you can is a delicious and educational experience. You get an opportunity to taste varietals, comparing texture, sweetness, flavor, and color. You will be able to make an informed decision about your purchase rather than hoping that the peach you selected tastes like a peach when you get it home! Lastly, don't be tempted to buy out of season fruit that has been shipped across the globe. It lacks flavor and freshness after its long journey and it is expensive.

NUTS Pound for pound, nuts can be an expensive ingredient to work with, but just a little goes a long way in frozen desserts. When toasting nuts, use a medium-hot oven (350°F) and toss the nuts repeatedly during the toasting process for even color. Deeply toast (but do not burn!) nuts, and grind them with a small amount of sugar in a food processor to release and capture their natural, flavorful oils. Freeze unused raw nuts to extend their shelf life or, better still, purchase only what is needed to ensure freshness.

ALCOHOL If you are anything like us, there is a decent liquor cabinet tucked away in your home. This makes for a boozy opportunity to flavor your creations with anywhere from a dash to a generous pour. When flavoring your bases, keep in mind that alcohol does not freeze, which is both good and bad for frozen desserts. The right amount of alcohol and the finished dessert is rendered complex and luscious; too much and the mixture will not properly set and will remain slushy and unappealing.

THE EQUIPMENT

A few essential kitchen utensils can streamline your ice cream–making preparations. Once you have the basics, you can begin to make quick work of even the most complex recipes.

First and foremost, of course, is the ice cream–making machine. The spectrum of brands and styles range from rudimentary (frozen cylinder, periodically hand churned) to vintage models relying on rock salt and ice to imported, self-contained freezing units that run into the thousands of dollars. While all make ice cream, not all ice creams are created equally.

ICE CREAM MAKER There are dozens of examples of ice cream makers crowding the market today, with varying degrees of ability, capacity, and results. At the low end of the spectrum are ice cream makers that operate using a metal canister, frozen in advance, and then filled with the ice cream or sherbet base. A blade is inserted into the canister and the entire bulky maker is periodically taken out of the freezer and churned manually until the dessert is frozen. The results are generally poor, and unless you have multiple canisters at the ready, you are limited to freezing one item per day.

For a nostalgic turn that produces fine results at a fairly reasonable price, a White Mountain brand ice cream maker consists of a white pine bucket, metal canister, dasher (blades), and either a hand crank or an electric motor. The bucket is filled with ice and sprinkled with rock salt, which produces a chemical reaction that drops the freezing point below 32°F. This enables rapid freezing. Combine the extremely low temperature with churning by hand or through the electric motor, and a quickly frozen smooth and creamy dessert is produced. As long as you have ice, rock salt, and extra canisters, perfectly simple ice cream is always within reach.

At the upper end of the price spectrum for the tabletop model of ice cream freezers is the Musso Lussino. It has a self-contained freezing mechanism and a metal dasher inside a 1½-quart stainless-steel bowl. With one moving part, a timer, freeze button, and churn button, making delicious frozen treats in about 30 minutes could not be easier. All the ice cream recipes in this book were created and tested using this machine.

From here, prices begin to skyrocket and veer into commercial-grade technology; they provide more control over air incorporation and variable churning speeds to yield highly professional results. If you have the budget, space, and desire you can have a gelateria-style product in your home, too!

There is other useful equipment to have on hand when making frozen desserts, in addition to the typical items you likely already have in your kitchen, such as containers with tight-fitting lids, heat-proof bowls (stainless steel is ideal), and heat-proof utensils, as well as a 4-quart electric mixer and a food processor.

FINE-MESH STRAINER This useful tool comes in handy when straining custard bases, as it easily filters out any undissolved sugar or cooked egg particles. Additionally, straining smooths purées and traps unwanted seeds while allowing maximum extraction from the fruit pulp. These strainers can be expensive, but they are long lasting and have multiple uses throughout the kitchen, thus justifying the cost.

HEAT-PROOF SPATULAS You will reach again and again for these silicone tools, so have at least three on hand. Opt for a brand that is heat resistant up to 500°F and has a single molded blade and handle construction to minimize areas where food can be trapped, potentially causing cross-contamination. Odor and stain resistant, dishwasher safe, and virtually indestructible, these spatulas are an ideal component for your ice cream production.

MICROPLANE ZESTER/GRATER A well-made kitchen tool, the Microplane has numerous applications and answers the call for all your grating needs. Bonus: It seemingly stays sharp indefinitely. Its ergonomically friendly handle will help you avoid the shredded knuckles your grandmother's old box grater routinely delivered. Remove citrus zest with ease from fruit both large and small, or grate whole spices, nuts, and even garlic and cheese.

SILPAT Rarely does restaurant-grade equipment cross over for use at home, but these silicone sheet pan liners are a revelation for amateur cooks. Reusable, nearly indestructible, and able to leap from the freezer to a 500°F oven in a single bound, these nonstick sheets can be used in place of parchment paper for a variety of baking tasks.

CANDY THERMOMETER Invest in a glass candy thermometer that has clear, legible type and measurements in both Fahrenheit and Celsius. A candy thermometer is imperative for deep-frying and for executing sugar work where maintaining specific temperatures is vital to a recipe's success.

MEASURING CUPS, LIQUID AND DRY If you do not already own a set of heat-proof Pyrex liquid measuring cups and stainless-steel dry measuring cups, invest in these before you embark on your first ice cream–making adventure. We provide precise measurements in our recipes, and these tools narrow the margin for error, where too much or too little of an ingredient can result in a gloppy mess.

ICE CREAM SCOOPS There are as many options in scoops as there are flavors to be scooped. We like the heavy industrial-grade stainless-steel scoops ranging in size from $2\frac{1}{2}$ teaspoons to $\frac{1}{4}$ cup. An oval scoop is a nice alternative to a sphere and useful when pairing multiple flavors of various intensities.

The United States tops the per-person ice cream consumption in the world with a whopping 48 pints per person per year! The United States is also the largest producer of ice cream.

techniques

Homemade ice cream and frozen desserts can be broken down into two equally important categories: the imaginative and the technical. Both types are uniquely challenging, rewarding, and fun, with the ultimate goal being a delicious treat to share with friends and family.

Making an ice cream, sherbet, or frozen yogurt base is nothing more than a fundamental series of steps that rely on a few rules, and even those can be bent from time to time. Once you understand the process, more attention can be paid to the creative aspects. Daring flavor combinations, elaborate sundaes, beautiful accompaniments, and festive desserts all spring from the foundational techniques you will learn throughout this book.

In this chapter, we'll outline the fundamental techniques needed for three beloved frozen desserts: ice cream, sherbet, and frozen yogurt. No matter the recipe, the base of each of these desserts is always the same. Understanding these steps will ensure that your foundation is strong—and thus give you the freedom to experiment with your own flavor combinations down the line. Quick equipment and ingredient overviews and essential troubleshooting tips round out the step-by-step instructions for each technique. You will find a lot more than ice cream, sherbet, and frozen yogurt recipes in this book, but these are the techniques you'll be turning to again and again throughout your ice cream education.

ICE CREAM

The basic ice cream custard base is essentially five ingredients: heavy cream, half-and-half, egg yolks, sugar, and salt. The trick to a perfect custard involves cooking the egg yolks with the dairy and sugar, stirring constantly, to 170°F, the temperature at which the protein in eggs begins to coagulate. This process gives the custard a rich, silky texture, also known as a *nappé* consistency.

The custard ultimately transforms into ice cream via freezing while churning, which prevents ice crystals from forming. Review these basic steps, equipment, ingredients, and tips for ice cream and be well on your way to the perfect ice cream base.

Equipment

* Heat-proof bowls (large, medium, and small)
* Heavy-bottomed 4-quart stainless-steel pot
* Liquid and dry measuring cups
* Heat-proof spatula
* Whisk
* Fine-mesh strainer
* Ice
* Ice cream maker
* 1- and 2-quart storage containers with tight-fitting lids

Basic Ingredients

* Heavy (whipping) cream
* Egg yolks
* Half-and-half
* Sugar
* Salt

MAKE THE BASE

1. Fill a large heat-proof bowl halfway with ice. Nestle a smaller heat-proof bowl in the ice and place a fine-mesh strainer over it. Add the heavy cream to the smaller of the chilled bowls. Set aside.

2. In a small heat-proof bowl, whisk the egg yolks to combine. Set aside.

3. In a heavy-bottomed 4-quart pot over medium-low heat, combine the half-and-half, sugar, and salt. Heat the mixture, stirring occasionally with a heat-proof spatula to dissolve the sugar and salt, until it is steamy and hot. Do not let the mixture boil.

4. When the sugar and salt are dissolved and the liquid is hot, temper the egg yolks by pouring about one-third of the hot liquid into the egg yolks in a slow, steady stream, whisking constantly.

5. Immediately pour the tempered egg yolks into the pot, whisking constantly to combine. Scrape out the bowl that contained the egg yolks, using a heat-proof spatula.

6. Lower the heat under the pot slightly, and use the spatula to stir and scrape the bottom and sides of the pot to keep the yolks from scrambling. Continue to gently cook the custard base, stirring constantly and adjusting the heat if necessary, until the base begins to thicken and evenly coats the spatula (see The Nappé Test, page 23).

7. Strain the custard into the chilled heavy cream. Do not scrape out the pot. Stir the mixture to stop the cooking process and to combine the custard and cream.

8. Thoroughly chill the base over the ice, or cover the bowl with plastic wrap and refrigerate for at least 2 hours, or preferably overnight.

THE NAPPÉ TEST

To test if your custard has reached the *nappé* state, dip a wooden spoon in the custard and drag your finger across it. If the thickened custard stays separated by the line you created with your finger, you have reached the *nappé* state. Quickly proceed with the straining and chilling steps before your custard overcooks. If the liquid is runny and thin and does not hold a streak for a second or two, you have not reached *nappé* consistency yet and the custard needs to continue cooking.

We generally do not use a thermometer to gauge the readiness of our bases because we have made thousands over the years and have developed an eye for perfectly cooked custard. Feel free to use a thermometer while stirring to assess the readiness of your base,

but we guarantee that within a few tries, you too will recognize the telltale signs and will rely on your newfound acumen.

FREEZE

9. Place a 2-quart container with a tight-fitting lid in the freezer to chill. Freeze the chilled base according to your ice cream maker's instructions. Store the finished ice cream in the chilled container.

A Note on Gelato

To say we love gelato is an understatement. So why would we exclude one of the greatest contributions Italian culture has bestowed upon global gastronomy? The truth is we believe authentic gelato cannot be fabricated at home. Until advances in retail ice cream machines include options for air control and variable churning speeds, gelato shall remain a product of the boutique gelateria. It would be disingenuous to refer to any of the ice creams in this book (scrumptious as they may be) as gelato. It is this gelato vacuum that compels us to visit Italy—or any Little Italy across this country—again and again. And again.

THE SCOOP

While making ice cream is a fairly simple task, several valuable tips can enhance the process and ensure great results every time. Here are a few commonsense hacks we have discovered over the years:

* If your custard base has overcooked (it will look slightly like scrambled eggs), transfer the cooled and strained base to a blender. Pulse it until it's smooth. This should take just a few pulses.

* To ensure maximum flavor in berry ice creams, start with equal parts sweetened purée and custard base. Add the custard base to the purée in small amounts, tasting it as you go. When the ice cream base is both creamy and bright with fruit flavor to your taste, stop adding the custard.

* If ice cream is left to churn in the machine too long, it may overprocess into butter. Unfortunately, once the fatty solids have separated, your ice cream is beyond rescue. Most modern freezing machines have a timer. Use it, or risk making a costly batch of sweetened butter.

* Too much alcohol in your custard base and it won't freeze? Empty the machine, remove ½ cup of the boozy base, and replace it with 1 cup of heavy (whipping) cream. Recombine, then proceed with freezing.

* Planning ahead is the key to successful ice cream preparation. Make space in your freezer to store your finished product, preferably in an upright position, and with room for cold air to circulate around the container. This will ensure quick and even freezing. Pre-freeze the container you are using to store your frozen dessert for at least 15 minutes before adding the finished ice cream to it, to prevent unnecessary melting.

* Before you start making the custard base, create a setup to instantly stop it from overcooking. Partially fill a large stainless-steel bowl with ice and nestle a medium bowl in the ice. Place a fine-mesh strainer over the medium bowl. To further guard against overcooking, add a portion of the recipe's dairy to the medium bowl. Once the custard base is finished, quickly strain it into the cold liquid. A quick stir of the liquid, and the cooking process is stopped and the custard is on its way to chilling.

* An oft-overlooked ingredient in ice cream preparation is salt. We are not referring to salt-based flavors that are wildly popular these days but to the sweet recipes where you might think salt would interfere with other flavors. Quite the contrary; we add a generous pinch of salt to fruit-based ice creams to enhance the flavors. In citrus sherbets, salt helps mute the citric acid, and in chocolate items it rounds out the complex cacao notes. Reach for the kosher salt the next time you are fashioning a frozen dessert base, and unlock hidden flavors.

* Unused custard base does not have to go to waste. Simply freeze the unchurned base and thaw it at a later date—this impacts the finished product very little. Allow the frozen custard base to thaw completely in your refrigerator overnight and then churn as usual in the ice cream maker.

* For maximum flavor extraction when using nuts as a flavor base in your ice cream custards, we suggest a deep, almost burnt

toasting in the oven followed by a long, slow steep in the dairy you will use to make the custard base. However, nuts are porous and can soak up a portion of your custard base, even with a hearty wringing out. If there has been significant loss to your custard after the steeping and straining steps, add a small amount of heavy cream to replace the absorbed base and guarantee a sufficient yield of finished ice cream.

* A perfect use for a Microplane grater is to capture the most flavorful part of the citrus zest while stopping just shy of the inner, usually bitter, pith that lies between fruit and skin. The exterior zest is full of aromatics and oils that flavor custards and sherbets fantastically. Capture these vital essences by grating the prescribed amount of zest directly over the sugar, which catches the oil and essence that would otherwise be lost.

* Our preferred method for separating eggs is as follows: Gather two bowls, one large and one small. Gently crack each egg into the large bowl, being careful not to fracture the yolk membrane. With a clean, dry hand, reach in and gently scoop up the yolk and allow the white to drain away through your fingers. Transfer the yolk to the smaller bowl, then repeat for the remaining eggs, one at a time. Use the separated whites for another purpose, such as in ice milk recipes or to make *Crispy Meringue Boats* (page 163).

SHERBET

Sherbet, or sorbet as it is sometimes known, packs all the refreshment and satisfaction of ice cream without the egg yolks and dairy of traditional custard. What you are left with is a slightly icy, intensely flavorful, sweetly balanced creation. Without question, sherbet lends its qualities to accenting the full spectrum of fresh fruit. The basic recipe for sherbets is a 4 to 1 ratio of fruit purée to sugar. From there it's a matter of adjusting the sweetness and acidity and adding flavorings to taste.

Equipment

* Food processor
* Liquid and dry measuring cups
* Whisk
* Fine-mesh strainer
* Ice cream maker
* 1- and 2-quart storage containers with tight-fitting lids

In 1846 Nancy Johnson patented the first hand-cranked ice cream freezer.

Basic Ingredients

* Fruit
* Sugar
* Kosher salt
* Optional: alcohol, water, freshly squeezed lemon juice

MAKE THE BASE

Purée the fruit in a food processor. For smoother purées or to trap unwanted seeds or peel, strain the purée.

Using a liquid measuring cup, measure the fruit purée to determine how much sugar to add.

Using a dry measuring cup, measure out one-quarter of the amount of fruit purée in granulated sugar and add this to the purée. For example, if you have 1 cup of purée, you will need $\frac{1}{4}$ cup of sugar. Add a generous pinch of salt to the purée, too. Stir to completely dissolve the sugar and salt. Taste the mixture and adjust accordingly with spirits, lemon juice, more salt, or water, if desired.

Chill the purée thoroughly in the refrigerator for at least 2 hours, or preferably overnight.

THE SCOOP

* If your fruit-based sherbet base lacks a final bright, flavorful note, add a few spoonfuls of like-minded fruit preserves or jam to accent the flavor. Additionally, when puréeing and straining berries, reserve a portion of the seeds and pulp to stir in prior to freezing.

* Lemon juice, when added to every variety of sherbet base, balances the natural sweetness of ripe, sugary fruits and rounds out the overall flavor. Use anywhere from a few drops up to several tablespoons, depending on individual tastes.

* Take care to purée fruits properly and thoroughly. One way to mar a delicious sherbet is to leave large chunks of unpuréed fruit in your sherbet. Large, potentially icy bits of unseasoned fruit can be strained through a medium-mesh strainer prior to spinning.

* Unlike custard-based ice cream, if you do not consume all the sherbet you have spun within 2 or 3 days of making it, you do not need to discard it for fear of it becoming too icy or gummy. Simply thaw the mixture overnight in the refrigerator and refreeze in your ice cream maker. This refreshes it, and you can continue to enjoy the frozen treat.

FREEZE

Place a 2-quart container with a tight-fitting lid in the freezer to chill. Freeze the purée according to your ice cream maker's instructions.

Store the finished sherbet in the chilled container. Ideally consume the sherbet within 2 to 3 days, but it will never be better than right out of the machine!

FROZEN YOGURT

Frozen yogurt—or fro yo—became popular in the United States in the 1980s. We think it's safe to say it's here to stay, and for good reason. It's a wonderful blend of creamy and tart.

Equipment

* Whisk
* Liquid and dry measuring cups
* Stainless-steel bowl
* Ice cream maker
* 1- and 2-quart storage containers with tight-fitting lids

Basic Ingredients

* Plain all-natural French-style yogurt
* Honey or sugar
* Vanilla bean or extract
* Kosher salt
* Optional: fruit purée

MAKE THE BASE

Sweeten the yogurt with honey or sugar by thoroughly whisking them together.

Stir in the vanilla and salt. Then adjust the yogurt base with selected flavorings and fruit purée (if using). Chill the yogurt base thoroughly in the refrigerator for at least 2 hours, or preferably overnight.

FREEZE

Place a 2-quart container with a tight-fitting lid in the freezer to chill. Freeze the yogurt base according to your ice cream maker's instructions.

Store the finished frozen yogurt in a container with a tight-fitting lid and that allows for easy scooping. Ideally consume the frozen yogurt within 2 to 3 days, but it will never be better than right out of the machine!

THE SCOOP

* The less there is to the frozen yogurt, the better your results will be. Seek out whole-milk, French-style yogurt, which tends to be slightly thinner than Greek-style; this is ideal for making fro yo. The yogurt you use should contain only two ingredients: milk and active live cultures. We are skeptical of yogurts with thickeners like gelatin and advise against using them to make frozen yogurt.

* Avoid flavored yogurts, even simple flavors like vanilla, as commercial vanilla can be of poor quality. We recommend plain yogurt for two simple reasons: you begin with a blank canvas and flavor it as you wish, and the yogurt's natural flavor won't compete with other added components.

* We never heat yogurt as we do the dairy used when making a custard-based ice cream. The goal for frozen yogurt is to retain the tangy brightness that yogurt provides, even when frozen. Heating the yogurt degrades that quality.

YOUR NEXT ICE CREAM SOCIAL

Enjoying ice cream and other frozen treats always tastes better when you're surrounded by friends and family. That's why the idea of an ice cream social is so universally enticing. If this is your inaugural fete, let us suggest a few themed ideas and menus to get you started. To satisfy a diverse crowd, you have to have a little something for everyone, from toddlers to grandparents. The wide range of flavors and textures throughout this book should satisfy even the pickiest of ice cream aficionados—though, to be honest, who can complain when presented with any freshly spun homemade ice cream?

We cherish the limited time we have to spend with family and friends and therefore go out of our way to fulfill special requests, or attend to dietary restrictions, especially for children.

Ice cream socials seem to go hand in hand with festive and joyous themes that match the revelry of the sweets. Draw inspiration from your guest list and design your menu around those in attendance. The youngest guests may have a bit of trouble devouring a large sundae, but an ice pop is manageable for children of all ages. Parents will appreciate a sophisticated offering, not too sweet, and maybe with a splash of festive booze.

Create a varied ice cream menu a few days before your party, and include at least one item that will please everyone. We like to shop in advance and purchase fruit early in case it needs a day or two longer to ripen. We often let the farmers' markets dictate our menus, especially in the summer when fruits and berries are local and at their peak ripeness.

One day before the event, have all your bases completed and ready to freeze. If you plan on serving three or four confections, it is wise to fully freeze at least two the night before so there is ample time for the ice creams to harden before guests arrive. Items like ice cream sandwiches can be made the morning of the event if the ice cream is spun the day before. Freshly baked cookies are never better than the day they are made, but assembled sandwiches need time in the freezer to solidify as well.

Think about activities that go hand in hand with a lively ice cream–themed event. If you are expecting a group of kids, set out a large array of Lego building blocks. In between slurping ice cream cones and ice pops, they can get creative.

Resurrect game night for the adult crowd and bookend a spirited competition with boozy concoctions. Create a buffet-style offering with a variety of sauces, toppings, and cones, artfully displayed, so guests can design their own indulgences. End the night with a strongly brewed espresso, poured over a variety of ice cream flavors such as Coffee Ice Cream (page 45), complex Gianduja Ice Cream (page 62), or the classic Madagascar Vanilla Ice Cream (page 34).

We scour flea markets and garage sales for antique ice cream serving utensils and vintage glassware. They can usually be had for cheap, especially if you find an incomplete set. Accent your party theme with forgotten, mismatched, and multi-shaped sundae coupes, split boats, and milkshake glasses. Relics of a bygone era, they will remind your guests of the spirit of the old-fashioned ice cream social, but with a modern twist.

Use the sample menus as inspiration and have fun! For parties of 10 to 15 guests, with two or three frozen offerings, we suggest 4 to 6 quarts of ice cream, sherbet, and/or frozen yogurt. For gatherings of 25 to 30 guests, with three or four frozen offerings, we recommend 5 to 8 quarts. Plan on each guest sampling at least one fountain-type drink, such as a milkshake or float. If serving cones, one per person should be sufficient.

FOR THE KIDS
ICE CREAM SOCIAL

Fresh strawberry Milkshakes (page 117)

Watermelon Ice Pops (page 152)

Cookies and Crema Ice Cream
(page 72) with sugar cones

Vanilla-Orange Sundae: Tangerine Sherbet
(page 88) and Madagascar Vanilla Ice Cream
(page 34) with Perfectly Whipped Cream
(page 207) and crumbled gingersnaps

EVERYONE LOVES A FAMILY
ICE CREAM SOCIAL

Plum Ice Cream (page 104)
with gingersnaps

Brown Cows (Root Beer Floats) (page 121)

Peanut Butter Ice Cream (page 134)
with sugar cones, rolled in All-American
Peanut Brittle (page 204)

Old-fashioned Banana Split (page 119)

THE ADULTS-ONLY
ICE CREAM SOCIAL

Eggnog Ice Cream (page 165)
drowned in fresh espresso

Rum-Raisin Ice Cream (page 176)
milkshakes with a float of aged rum

Grapefruit Sherbet with Campari
and Candied Grapefruit (page 181)

Bittersweet Chocolate Sherbet (page 76)
and Toasted Almond Ice Cream (page 43)
sundaes with Roasted Cherries (page 216)

CHAPTER THREE

classic

What makes a classic a classic? For starters, it must be universally loved and timeless, though it can be a new creation—an instant classic, if you will. When flavors or preparations span several decades or, more importantly, generations, you know you have a classic on your hands. We tried to compile a list of perfectly simple classics anyone could turn to, whether entertaining discerning palates or a group of ice cream–loving kids.

MADAGASCAR VANILLA
ICE CREAM

MAKES 2 QUARTS * PREP/COOK TIME: 30 MINUTES, PLUS CHILLING AND FREEZING

The essence of vanilla beans from Madagascar, exotic and heady, combined with creamy dairy makes for the world's most popular ice cream flavor. This ice cream is foundational to many of the recipes in this book. Omit the vanilla bean and you are left with a versatile custard base. Master this basic technique and you are well on your way to making perfectly simple ice cream every time!

4 cups heavy (whipping) cream

12 extra-large egg yolks

2½ cups half-and-half

1⅓ cups sugar

Generous pinch kosher salt

1 Madagascar vanilla bean (optional)

MAKE THE BASE

Fill a large heat-proof bowl halfway with ice. Nestle a smaller heat-proof bowl in the ice and place a fine-mesh strainer over it. Add the heavy cream to the smaller of the chilled bowls. Set aside.

In a medium heat-proof bowl, whisk the egg yolks to combine. Set aside.

In a heavy-bottomed 4-quart pot over medium-low heat, combine the half-and-half, sugar, and salt. Heat the mixture, stirring occasionally with a heat-proof spatula to dissolve the sugar and salt, until it is steamy and hot. Do not allow the mixture to boil. Meanwhile, with a paring knife, split the vanilla bean (if using) lengthwise, scrape out the seeds, and add the pod and seeds to the warming liquid.

When the liquid is hot, temper the egg yolks by pouring 1 cup of the hot liquid into the yolks in a slow, steady stream, whisking constantly. Immediately pour the tempered yolks into the pot, whisking constantly to combine. Scrape out the bowl that contained the egg yolks, using a heat-proof spatula.

Lower the heat under the pot slightly, and use the spatula to stir and scrape the bottom of the pot to keep the yolks from scrambling. Continue to gently cook the custard base, stirring constantly and adjusting the heat if necessary, until the base begins to thicken and evenly coats the spatula. This should take about 5 minutes.

Strain the custard into the chilled heavy cream. Do not scrape out the pot. Stir the mixture to stop the cooking process and,

if you desire, add the strained vanilla pod to the custard. Thoroughly chill the base over the ice, or cover the bowl with plastic wrap and refrigerate for at least 2 hours, or preferably overnight.

FREEZE

Place a 2-quart container with a tight-fitting lid in the freezer to chill. Remove the vanilla pod (if still in the base). Freeze the chilled base according to your ice cream maker's instructions. Store the finished ice cream in the chilled container.

STRAWBERRY
ICE CREAM

MAKES 1½ QUARTS * PREP/COOK TIME: 30 MINUTES, PLUS CHILLING AND FREEZING

Strawberry ice cream appears in a variety of desserts throughout this book; master this technique and it will unlock a host of recipes. Since the sweetness of strawberries can vary widely, you will need to taste, and taste again, to get the flavor of your finished base perfectly balanced. Enhance the flavor with a few drops of Kirschwasser or framboise and leave some seeds in the mix for texture.

2 cups heavy (whipping) cream

6 extra-large egg yolks

1¼ cups half-and-half

⅔ cup sugar, plus more if needed

Generous pinch kosher salt

2 pints strawberries

1 teaspoon pure vanilla extract

1 tablespoon freshly squeezed lemon juice

Kirschwasser or framboise (optional)

MAKE THE BASE

Fill a large heat-proof bowl halfway with ice. Nestle a smaller heat-proof bowl in the ice and place a fine-mesh strainer over it. Add the heavy cream to the smaller of the chilled bowls. Set aside.

In a small heat-proof bowl, whisk the egg yolks to combine. Set aside.

In a heavy bottomed 2-quart saucepot over medium-low heat, combine the half-and-half, sugar, and salt. Heat the mixture, stirring occasionally with a heat-proof spatula to dissolve the sugar and salt, until it is steamy and hot. Do not allow the mixture to boil.

When the liquid is hot, temper the egg yolks by pouring 1 cup of the hot liquid into the yolks in a slow, steady stream, whisking constantly. Immediately pour the tempered yolks into the pot, whisking constantly to combine. Scrape out the bowl that contained the egg yolks, using a heat-proof spatula. >>

Lower the heat under the pot slightly, and use the spatula to stir and scrape the bottom of the pot to keep the yolks from scrambling. Continue to gently cook the custard base, stirring constantly and adjusting the heat if necessary, until the base begins to thicken and evenly coats the spatula. This should take about 5 minutes.

Strain the custard into the chilled heavy cream. Do not scrape out the pot. Stir the mixture to stop the cooking process and to combine the custard and cream. Thoroughly chill the base over the ice, or cover the bowl with plastic wrap and refrigerate for at least 2 hours, or preferably overnight.

Wash, dry, and hull the strawberries. Transfer them to a food processor and purée until smooth. Strain the purée and reserve 1 tablespoon of the seeds and pulp. There should be about $1\frac{1}{2}$ cups of purée.

Add an equal amount of the thoroughly chilled custard base (about $1\frac{1}{2}$ cups) to the strawberry purée. Stir in the vanilla extract, salt, and a few drops each of lemon juice and Kirschwasser (if using). Taste the base and adjust the flavors, if needed, with a teaspoon of sugar, more lemon juice, or more custard base. Ideally, the finished base will be a creamy strawberry blend, a mix of bright and sweet. You may not need to use the entire custard base, depending on the flavor intensity of your strawberries. Stir in the seeds and pulp.

FREEZE

Place a 2-quart container with a tight-fitting lid in the freezer to chill. Freeze the base according to your ice cream maker's instructions. Store the finished ice cream in the chilled container.

 tip Framboise is a high-proof *eau-de-vie* distilled with raspberries. It adds a wonderful dimension to all manner of berry desserts.

MINT CHOCOLATE CHIP
ICE CREAM

MAKES 2 QUARTS * PREP/COOK TIME: 45 MINUTES, PLUS CHILLING AND FREEZING

The cool combination of mint essence and chocolaty-chocolate flecks is ageless, though this version lacks the Day-Glo green color of commercial mint chip ice creams. Featuring a blend of peppermint extract and fresh herbs, this ice cream is so full flavored that we bet no one will miss the artificial coloring.

8 ounces bittersweet chocolate, chopped

1 bunch fresh mint

1⅓ cups sugar, divided

4 cups heavy (whipping) cream

2½ cups half-and-half

Generous pinch kosher salt

12 extra-large egg yolks

1 teaspoon pure peppermint extract

PREP

In a double boiler or small stainless-steel bowl set over a pot of barely simmering water, melt the chocolate.

Line a rimmed baking sheet with parchment paper or a silicone baking mat and pour the melted chocolate onto the sheet. Use an offset spatula to spread the chocolate very thinly and evenly. Place the pan in the refrigerator until ready to use.

Pick the mint leaves from the stems and place the leaves in a food processor with ⅓ cup of sugar. Grind the ingredients to a fine, grainy purée.

MAKE THE BASE

Fill a large heat-proof bowl halfway with ice. Nestle a smaller heat-proof bowl in the ice and place a fine-mesh strainer over it. Add the heavy cream to the smaller of the chilled bowls. Set aside. >>

In a heavy bottomed 4-quart pot over medium-low heat, combine the half-and-half, mint-sugar purée, remaining 1 cup of sugar, and the salt, stirring occasionally with a heat-proof spatula to dissolve the sugar and salt, until it is steamy and hot. Do not allow the mixture to boil. When the liquid is hot, remove it from the heat and set it aside to steep for 15 minutes.

Meanwhile, in a medium heat-proof bowl, whisk the egg yolks to combine. Set aside.

Return the pot to the heat and rewarm the steeped mixture. When the liquid is hot, temper the egg yolks by pouring 1 cup of the hot liquid into the yolks in a slow, steady stream, whisking constantly. Immediately pour the tempered yolks into the pot, whisking constantly to combine. Scrape out the bowl that contained the yolks, using a heat-proof spatula.

Lower the heat under the pot slightly, and use the spatula to stir and scrape the bottom of the pot to keep the yolks from scrambling. Continue to gently cook the custard base, stirring constantly and adjusting the heat if necessary, until the base begins to thicken and evenly coats the spatula. This should take about 5 minutes.

Strain the custard into the chilled heavy cream. Do not scrape out the pot, and do not press on the strained mint to extract more custard base as it may be slightly bitter. Stir the mixture to stop the cooking process and to combine the custard and cream. Thoroughly chill the base over the ice, or cover with plastic wrap and refrigerate for at least 2 hours, or preferably overnight. Stir the peppermint extract into the chilled ice cream.

Remove the chocolate from the refrigerator and break or chop it into bite-size shards.

FREEZE

Place a 2-quart container with a tight-fitting lid in the freezer to chill. Freeze the base according to your ice cream maker's instructions. Evenly fold the chocolate shards into the frozen ice cream so there is chocolate in every bite. Store the finished ice cream in the chilled container.

CARAMEL
ICE CREAM

MAKES 2 QUARTS ✳ PREP/COOK TIME: 20 MINUTES, PLUS CHILLING AND FREEZING

The rich and edgy flavor of this caramel ice cream is indeed surprising. The key is to bring the caramelizing sugar to the point just before it's burnt. The result is a deep caramel flavor that is not too sweet. The darker you get the caramel, the less sweet it becomes. We have to tip our hat to our colleague Patricia Salvati, a master caramel ice cream maker, for the inspiration for this recipe.

2½ cups sugar, plus 2 to 3 tablespoons for seasoning adjustment

4½ cups heavy (whipping) cream

2¼ cups half-and-half

12 extra-large egg yolks

¼ teaspoon kosher salt

¾ teaspoon pure vanilla extract

PREP

Heat the sugar in a heavy-bottomed, 4-quart pot over medium heat. Using a long-handled heat-proof spatula or wooden spoon, occasionally stir the sugar so that it is melting uniformly, mixing in any dry sugar as it cooks. Have your cream close by; you will be adding it immediately once the caramel is ready. (Also have a small bowl of ice water next to you—if any caramel splatters on your fingers, you can plunge them right in.)

Continue to cook the sugar for 5 to 8 minutes, monitoring its color. As the sugar darkens, it will begin to smoke and foam up a bit. (If you like your caramel ice cream on the "edgy" side, let the caramel foam for a couple more seconds.) At this point, slowly pour the heavy cream into the caramel, stirring with your spatula or wooden spoon, until the caramel and cream are completely mixed together. Set aside. >>

MAKE THE BASE

Fill a large heat-proof bowl halfway with ice. Nestle a smaller heat-proof bowl in the ice and place a fine-mesh strainer over it. Add the half-and-half to the smaller of the chilled bowls. Set aside.

In a small heat-proof bowl, whisk the egg yolks to combine. Set aside.

Place the pot with the caramel over medium heat. When the liquid is hot, temper the egg yolks by pouring 1 cup of the hot liquid into the egg yolks in a slow, steady stream, whisking constantly. Immediately pour the tempered yolks into the pot, whisking constantly to combine. Scrape out the bowl that contained the egg yolks, using a heat-proof spatula.

Lower the heat under the pot slightly, and use the spatula to stir and scrape the bottom of the pot to keep the yolks from scrambling. Continue to gently cook the custard base, stirring constantly and adjusting the heat if necessary, until the base begins to thicken and evenly coats the spatula. This should take about 5 minutes.

Strain the custard into the chilled half-and-half. Do not scrape out the pot. Stir the mixture to stop the cooking process and to combine the custard and half-and-half. Thoroughly chill the base over the ice, or cover the bowl with plastic wrap and refrigerate for at least 2 hours, or preferably overnight.

Taste the chilled base and adjust it for sweetness. If the caramel is quite dark, more sugar may be needed. Stir in the salt and vanilla.

FREEZE

Place a 2-quart container with a tight-fitting lid in the freezer to chill. Freeze the chilled base according to your ice cream maker's instructions. Store the finished ice cream in the chilled container.

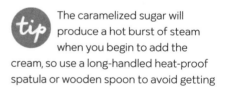

tip The caramelized sugar will produce a hot burst of steam when you begin to add the cream, so use a long-handled heat-proof spatula or wooden spoon to avoid getting a steam burn on your hand and wrist.

TOASTED ALMOND
ICE CREAM

MAKES 2 QUARTS * PREP/COOK TIME: 1½ HOURS, PLUS CHILLING AND FREEZING

Toasted nuts make for first-rate ice creams. The oils and almost burnt essence released from roasting nuts easily permeates custard bases that are steeped with them. Dark-roasting the nuts is a necessity to create a full-flavored ice cream, as the full nuttiness is dulled by freezing. What you get is the true nut flavor, frozen in place.

2 cups whole raw almonds

1⅓ cups sugar, divided

4 cups heavy (whipping) cream

2½ cups half-and-half

Generous pinch kosher salt

12 extra-large egg yolks

1 tablespoon Frangelico (optional)

PREP

Preheat the oven to 325°F.

Spread the almonds in a single layer on a rimmed baking sheet. Toast them until they are deep brown (but not burnt), about 20 minutes. Set them aside to cool slightly.

Combine the nuts and ⅓ cup of sugar in a food processor and process until they are finely ground. Transfer the nut-sugar mixture to a heavy-bottomed 4-quart pot.

MAKE THE BASE

Fill a large heat-proof bowl halfway with ice. Nestle a smaller heat-proof bowl in the ice and place a fine-mesh strainer over it. Add the heavy cream to the smaller of the chilled bowls. Set aside.

Add the half-and-half, the remaining 1 cup of sugar, and the salt to the pot. Over medium-low heat, heat the mixture, stirring >>

occasionally with a heat-proof spatula to dissolve the sugar and salt, until it is steamy and hot. Do not allow the mixture to boil. When the liquid is hot, remove the pot from the heat, cover it, and set it aside for 1 hour to steep the nuts in the liquid.

In a small heat-proof bowl, whisk the egg yolks to combine. Set aside.

Return the almond custard base to the stove and reheat it over medium-low heat. Once the liquid is hot, temper the egg yolks by pouring 1 cup of the hot liquid into the yolks in a slow, steady stream, whisking constantly. Immediately pour the tempered yolks into the pot, whisking constantly to combine. Scrape out the bowl that contained the egg yolks, using a heat-proof spatula.

Lower the heat under the pot slightly, and use the spatula to stir and scrape the bottom of the pot to keep the yolks from scrambling. Continue to gently cook the custard base, stirring constantly and adjusting the heat if

necessary, until the base begins to thicken and evenly coats the spatula. This should take about 5 minutes.

Strain the custard into the chilled heavy cream. Do not scrape out the pot. Stir the mixture to stop the cooking process, and use the spatula or the back of a spoon to press the strained almonds to extract as much liquid as possible. Stir the Frangelico (if using) into the custard base. Thoroughly chill the base over the ice, or cover the bowl with plastic wrap and refrigerate for at least 2 hours, or preferably overnight.

FREEZE

Place a 2-quart container with a tight-fitting lid in the freezer to chill. Freeze the chilled base according to your ice cream maker's instructions. Store the finished ice cream in the chilled container.

COFFEE
ICE CREAM

MAKES 2 QUARTS * PREP/COOK TIME: 30 MINUTES, PLUS CHILLING AND FREEZING

Coffee ice cream ranks as a top ten favorite flavor the world over, and for good reason. Sweetened cream combined with the robust flavor of roasted coffee beans creates a dreamy marriage. The rich coffee flavor wonderfully complements obvious choices like chocolate, toasted nuts, and caramel, but try pairing it with a flavorful chocolate sherbet for a change of pace. Wonderful sandwiched between Chocolate Wafer Cookies (page 217) or as the headliner in an *affogato mocha* ("drowned" in espresso), coffee ice cream is as versatile as it is delicious.

¼ cup decaffeinated espresso beans

2 cups half-and-half

1 cup sugar, plus more for seasoning adjustment

3 cups heavy (whipping) cream

9 extra-large egg yolks

Few drops pure vanilla extract

Kosher salt, for seasoning adjustment

PREP

Tear off a large sheet of parchment paper, roughly 10 by 10 inches. Place the espresso beans on half of the paper and fold over the parchment to cover the beans. Using a rolling pin, gently roll over the beans to carefully crush them. Avoid pulverizing them.

In a heavy-bottomed 4-quart pot over medium-high heat, heat the half-and-half and sugar until steamy and hot, stirring frequently to dissolve the sugar. Remove the pot from the heat. Add the crushed espresso beans to the pot, cover the pot with a tight-fitting lid, and steep the mixture for 15 minutes.

MAKE THE BASE

Fill a large heat-proof bowl halfway with ice. Nestle a smaller heat-proof bowl in the ice and place a fine-mesh strainer over it. Add the heavy cream to the smaller of the chilled bowls. Set aside.

In a small heat-proof bowl, whisk the egg yolks to combine. Set aside. >>

Return the steeped custard base to the stove and reheat it over medium-low heat. Once the liquid is hot, temper the egg yolks by pouring 1 cup of the hot liquid into the yolks in a slow, steady stream, whisking constantly. Immediately pour the tempered yolks into the pot, whisking constantly to combine. Scrape out the bowl that contained the egg yolks, using a heat-proof spatula.

Lower the heat under the pot slightly, and use the spatula to stir and scrape the bottom of the pot to keep the yolks from scrambling. Continue to gently cook the custard base, stirring constantly and adjusting the heat if necessary, until the base begins to thicken and evenly coats the spatula. This should take about 5 minutes.

Strain the custard into the chilled heavy cream. Do not scrape out the pot. Stir the mixture to stop the cooking process, and use the spatula or the back of a spoon to press the strained espresso beans to extract as much liquid as possible. Stir the vanilla into the custard base. Taste the custard and adjust the sweetness level, if needed, with a little more sugar or a pinch of kosher salt. Thoroughly chill the base over the ice, or cover the bowl with plastic wrap and refrigerate for at least 2 hours, or preferably overnight.

FREEZE

Place a 2-quart container with a tight-fitting lid in the freezer to chill. Freeze the chilled base according to your ice cream maker's instructions. Store the finished ice cream in the chilled container.

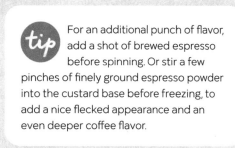

tip For an additional punch of flavor, add a shot of brewed espresso before spinning. Or stir a few pinches of finely ground espresso powder into the custard base before freezing, to add a nice flecked appearance and an even deeper coffee flavor.

BANANA-WALNUT
ICE CREAM

MAKES 2 QUARTS * PREP/COOK TIME: 30 MINUTES, PLUS CHILLING AND FREEZING

Banana-walnut ice cream is one of our all-time favorites. This recipe makes perfect use of those slightly overripe bananas on your counter. The fragrant, creamy banana purée lends a lovely texture to this ice cream, as does the crunch of the walnut pieces.

3 cups heavy (whipping) cream

8 extra-large egg yolks

1½ cups half-and-half

1¼ cups sugar, divided

4 large overripe bananas

½ teaspoon pure vanilla extract

Generous pinch kosher salt

1 cup walnuts

MAKE THE BASE

Fill a large heat-proof bowl halfway with ice. Nestle a smaller heat-proof bowl in the ice and place a fine-mesh strainer over it. Add the heavy cream to the smaller of the chilled bowls. Set aside.

In a small heat-proof bowl, whisk the egg yolks to combine. Set aside.

In a heavy-bottomed 4-quart pot over medium-low heat, combine the half-and-half and 1 cup of sugar. Heat the mixture, stirring occasionally with a heat-proof spatula to dissolve the sugar, until it is steamy and hot. Do not allow the mixture to boil.

When the liquid is hot, temper the egg yolks by pouring 1 cup of the hot liquid into the yolks in a slow, steady stream, whisking constantly. Immediately pour the tempered yolks into the pot, whisking constantly to combine. Scrape out the bowl that contained the egg yolks, using a heat-proof spatula.

Lower the heat under the pot slightly, and use the spatula to stir and scrape the bottom of the pot to keep the yolks from scrambling. Continue to gently cook the custard base, stirring constantly and adjusting the heat if necessary, until the base begins to thicken and evenly coats the spatula. This should take about 5 minutes.

Strain the custard into the chilled heavy cream. Do not scrape out the pot. Stir the mixture to stop the cooking process and to combine the custard and cream. Thoroughly chill the base over the ice, or cover the bowl with plastic wrap and refrigerate for at least 2 hours, or preferably overnight.

In a food processor, purée the bananas with the remaining $\frac{1}{4}$ cup of sugar. This should make about $2\frac{2}{3}$ cups of purée. Set aside.

When the custard is chilled, add the banana purée, vanilla, and salt and mix thoroughly.

FREEZE

Place a 2-quart container with a tight-fitting lid in the freezer to chill. Freeze the chilled base according to your ice cream maker's instructions.

TOAST THE WALNUTS

While the base is freezing, toast the walnuts. Preheat the oven to 350°F.

Line a baking sheet with parchment paper or a silicone baking mat, and lay out the walnuts on the sheet in a single layer. Toast the walnuts, occasionally giving them a stir, until crispy, 12 to 14 minutes. Once they are cool enough to handle, rub them between your fingers and palms to loosen any skin that wants to come off. Walnut skins can be bitter, so this is an important step. Roughly chop the walnuts.

Fold the walnuts into the finished ice cream as you are filling your chilled storage container.

 If you have overripe bananas but aren't ready to make ice cream, purée them with the sugar and pop the purée into the freezer. The night before you make the ice cream, thaw the purée in the refrigerator so it's ready to use.

TOASTED COCONUT
ICE MILK

MAKES 1 QUART * PREP/COOK TIME: 1 HOUR, 15 MINUTES, PLUS FREEZING

Some of our favorite flavors are tropical in nature; they blend and complement each other, yet remain distinct. This stripped-down ice milk is a clear example of a bold tropical flavor. Press the coconut solids when straining them to extract as much flavor as possible, then pair this ice milk with complementary frozen delights such as Pineapple Sherbet (page 87) or Toasted Coconut Ice Cream (page 93).

1½ cups shredded coconut

2⅔ cups canned coconut milk (see the Tip)

1⅓ cups whole milk

¾ cup sugar, plus 2 tablespoons, divided

Generous pinch kosher salt

3 extra-large egg whites, at room temperature

PREP

Preheat the oven to 325°F.

Line a baking sheet with parchment paper or a silicone baking mat, and spread the shredded coconut on it in a single layer. Toast the coconut, giving it an occasional stir, for 5 to 7 minutes.

In a heavy-bottomed 2-quart pot over medium-low heat, combine the coconut milk, whole milk, toasted coconut, ¾ cup of sugar, and the salt, stirring occasionally with a heat-proof spatula to dissolve the sugar and salt. Do not allow the mixture to boil. When the sugar is dissolved and the milk is hot, remove the pot from the heat, cover it, and set it aside for 1 hour to steep the coconut.

MAKE THE BASE

Fill a large heat-proof bowl halfway with ice. Nestle a smaller heat-proof bowl in the ice and place a fine-mesh strainer over it.

Return the pot to the stove and reheat the liquid over medium heat. When it is hot, strain it into the smaller of the chilled bowls. Use the spatula or the back of a spoon to press the coconut to extract as much liquid as possible. Discard the coconut. Thoroughly chill the base over the ice, or cover the bowl with plastic wrap and refrigerate for at least 2 hours, or preferably overnight.

Whisk the egg whites to stiff peaks, either by hand in a clean, dry stainless-steel bowl, or using a standing electric mixer with the whisk attachment. When the whites begin to hold soft peaks, gradually add 1 tablespoon sugar and continue to whisk. Add the remaining tablespoon of sugar and continue to whisk the whites until they are shiny and stiff.

Using a spatula, gently fold the egg whites into the chilled milk.

FREEZE

Place a 2-quart container with a tight-fitting lid in the freezer to chill. Freeze the chilled base according to your ice cream maker's instructions. Store the finished ice milk in the chilled container.

 Canned coconut milk separates into thick cream and coconut water. Be sure to give it a good shake or whisk it together before using it. For this recipe, do not use the coconut milk or coconut water that comes in a carton in the dairy aisle.

ESPRESSO
GRANITA

MAKES 3 CUPS * PREP TIME: 5 MINUTES, PLUS FREEZING

Espresso—the rich, concentrated, slightly bitter coffee—jump-starts millions of Italians at least twice a day. Drop into any café, stride up to the bar, and within seconds you have a saucer with a small cup of *crema*-topped coffee to savor. So fast, so inexpensive, and so satisfying, which goes for our espresso granita as well. Layer this ice with Perfectly Whipped Cream (page 207) and you have a perfect, not-too-sweet ending to any meal.

1 cup brewed espresso, about 4 or 5 shots, chilled

3 teaspoons sugar

Generous pinch kosher salt

½ teaspoon cognac (optional)

MAKE THE BASE

Place an 8-by-12-inch glass or metal baking pan in the freezer to chill. The pan should rest flat on an easily accessible spot.

In a small bowl, stir together the espresso, sugar, and salt until the sugar and salt are completely dissolved. Stir in the cognac (if using).

FREEZE

Remove the chilled baking pan from the freezer and pour in the liquid. Return the pan to the freezer. After 30 minutes, use a fork to stir the granita from the outside in, stirring any ice crystals back into the liquid. Return the pan to the freezer. Repeat this step every 30 minutes for at least 3 hours, or until the entire mixture has frozen and has a uniformly light, "dry," crystalline texture. When the granita has reached this stage, cover it tightly with plastic wrap until you are ready to serve.

HOKEY POKEY
ICE CREAM

Toffee is the cooked, crunchy marriage of butter and sugar. It is usually eaten as a candy, but we like to fold it into ice cream for a snappy surprise. In New Zealand they fold toffee into vanilla ice cream and refer to it as hokey pokey. The name alone made us want to make some! In the United States, hokey pokey was an inexpensive portion of ice cream sold from a pushcart by Italian immigrants in the 1800s. Walking the streets, vendors would cry *"O che poco,"* or "Oh how little," which refers to the price of the frozen treat. Say it fast and you can see how it gradually came to be known as hokey pokey.

 A candy thermometer is not necessary to make a successful batch of toffee. You just need to observe the color as the sugar caramelizes, taking it off the heat when it is the correct color. If you want it a bit darker after you take it off the heat and while it is still in the pot, simply return the pot to the heat and cook it a little longer.

FOR THE TOFFEE

½ cup (1 stick) unsalted butter

½ cup sugar

Generous pinch kosher salt

2 ounces finely chopped bittersweet or semisweet chocolate (optional)

½ cup chopped, toasted nuts, such as pecans, almonds, or walnuts (optional)

FOR THE ICE CREAM

4 cups heavy (whipping) cream

12 extra-large egg yolks

2½ cups half-and-half

1⅓ cups sugar

Generous pinch kosher salt

MAKE THE TOFFEE

To make the toffee, line a baking sheet pan with parchment paper or a silicone baking mat, and set aside.

In a heavy-bottomed 2-quart pot, combine the butter, sugar, and salt over medium-high heat and allow the butter and sugar to melt. Cook the toffee, stirring occasionally, until it is a dark amber color. This is the hard-crack stage, 285°F on a candy thermo-meter. When it has reached this stage, turn off the heat and stir it for a minute as it begins to cool to work in any butter not already incorporated. >>

Pour the toffee onto the lined baking sheet and allow it to cool a bit. While it is still quite warm, sprinkle the chopped chocolate (if using) on top and, as it melts, use a metal offset spatula to spread it evenly across the toffee. Sprinkle on the chopped nuts (if using).

Place the baking sheet in the refrigerator to set the chocolate. Once completely chilled, break the toffee into pieces and store in an airtight container until you are ready to use it. This makes about 1 pound of toffee.

MAKE THE BASE

To make the ice cream base, fill a large heat-proof bowl halfway with ice. Nestle a smaller heat-proof bowl in the ice and place a fine-mesh strainer over it. Add the heavy cream to the smaller of the chilled bowls. Set aside.

In a small heat-proof bowl, whisk the egg yolks to combine. Set aside.

In a heavy-bottomed 4-quart pot over medium-low heat, combine the half-and-half, sugar, and salt. Heat the mixture, stirring occasionally with a heat-proof spatula to dissolve the sugar and salt, until it is steamy and hot. Do not allow the mixture to boil.

When the liquid is hot, temper the egg yolks by pouring 1 cup of the hot liquid into the yolks in a slow, steady stream, whisking constantly. Immediately pour the tempered yolks into the pot, whisking constantly to combine. Scrape out the bowl that contained the egg yolks, using a heat-proof spatula.

Lower the heat under the pot slightly, and use the spatula to stir and scrape the bottom of the pot to keep the yolks from scrambling. Continue to gently cook the custard base, stirring constantly and adjusting the heat if necessary, until the base begins to thicken and evenly coats the spatula. This should take about 5 minutes.

Strain the custard into the chilled heavy cream. Do not scrape out the pot. Stir the mixture to stop the cooking process and to combine the custard and cream. Thoroughly chill the base over the ice, or cover the bowl with plastic wrap and refrigerate for at least 2 hours, or preferably overnight.

FREEZE

Place a 2-quart container with a tight-fitting lid in your freezer to chill. Freeze the chilled base according to your ice cream maker's instructions.

Chop enough of the cooled toffee into bite-size pieces to yield $1\frac{1}{2}$ cups. Fold the chopped toffee into the finished ice cream as you are filling the chilled storage container.

BUTTERSCOTCH
ICE CREAM

MAKES 2 QUARTS * PREP/COOK TIME: 30 MINUTES, PLUS CHILLING AND FREEZING

The origins of the word *butterscotch* are a bit of a mystery. Some say it comes from the word *scotched,* because the hard candy version is difficult to break once it is cooled and therefore must be scored while still warm to portion. It may also come from the word *scorch,* whereby the sugar is cooked to the hard-crack stage, which is quite dark. Either way, we love it plain or with lots of toasted nuts and whipped cream. You could go crazy and drizzle it with warm Butterscotch Sauce (page 200), too!

1½ cups half-and-half

3 cups heavy (whipping) cream, divided

8 extra-large egg yolks

6 tablespoons unsalted butter

1 packed cup dark brown sugar

MAKE THE BASE

Fill a large heat-proof bowl halfway with ice. Nestle a smaller heat-proof bowl in the ice and place a fine-mesh strainer over it. Add the half-and-half and $1\frac{1}{2}$ cups of heavy cream to the smaller of the chilled bowls. Set aside.

In a small heat-proof bowl, whisk the egg yolks to combine. Set aside.

In a heavy-bottomed 4-quart pot over medium heat, melt the butter and then add the brown sugar. Stir until the sugar is moistened evenly.

Add the remaining $1\frac{1}{2}$ cups of heavy cream to the sugar mixture and heat it gently, stirring occasionally with a heat-proof spatula to dissolve the sugar, until it is steamy and hot. Do not let the mixture boil.

When the liquid is hot, temper the egg yolks by pouring 1 cup of the hot liquid into the yolks in a slow, steady stream, whisking constantly. Immediately pour the tempered yolks into the pot, whisking constantly to combine. Scrape out the bowl that contained the egg yolks, using a heat-proof spatula. >>

Lower the heat under the pot slightly, and use the spatula to stir and scrape the bottom of the pot to keep the yolks from scrambling. Continue to gently cook the custard base, stirring constantly and adjusting the heat if necessary, until the base begins to thicken and evenly coats the spatula. This should take about 5 minutes.

Strain the custard into the chilled cream and half-and-half. Do not scrape the pot. Stir the mixture to stop the cooking and to combine the liquids. Thoroughly chill the base over the ice, or cover the bowl with plastic wrap and refrigerate for at least 2 hours, or preferably overnight.

FREEZE

Place a 2-quart container with a tight-fitting lid in the freezer to chill. Freeze the chilled base according to your ice cream maker's instructions. Store the finished ice cream in the chilled container.

While we prefer to use dark brown sugar, in a pinch you can use light brown sugar and 2 tablespoons molasses. Brown sugar is simply a soft sugar product containing naturally occurring residual molasses, packaged as natural brown sugar. It is also produced commercially by adding molasses to refined white sugar.

BANANA
FROZEN YOGURT

MAKES 2 QUARTS * PREP TIME: 15 MINUTES, PLUS CHILLING AND FREEZING

Move over banana bread! There may be a no more delicious, healthy dessert than a purée of overripe bananas blended with yogurt and spun to perfection. It also couldn't be easier to make. This frozen yogurt also makes a great creamy ice pop.

5 overripe bananas

1 cup sugar, plus more if needed

5 tablespoons freshly squeezed orange or tangerine juice

5 cups plain whole-milk French-style yogurt

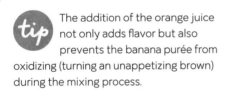

tip The addition of the orange juice not only adds flavor but also prevents the banana purée from oxidizing (turning an unappetizing brown) during the mixing process.

MAKE THE BASE

Slice each banana into 8 pieces. Place the fruit in a large bowl and add the sugar and the orange juice. Using an immersion blender, purée the mixture until it is very smooth.

Add the yogurt to the bowl and use a wooden spoon to mix everything together until well combined.

Taste the base and add a teaspoon or two more sugar if the bananas lack sweetness. Cover the bowl with plastic wrap and refrigerate the base to chill thoroughly for at least 2 hours, or preferably overnight.

FREEZE

Place a 2-quart container with a tight-fitting lid in the freezer to chill. Freeze the chilled base according to your ice cream maker's instructions. Store the finished frozen yogurt in the chilled container.

CHAPTER FOUR

chocolaty

Perhaps there is no single ingredient the world over that means so much to so many of us. Historically, entire economies rose and fell on chocolate production, fueled by skyrocketing New World demand and open trade routes. Cacao production dates to early pre-Columbian civilizations, with origins of the pod traced to the upper Amazon region. Thankfully, we live in an age where the refinement of chocolate production has reached such a high degree that today we experience the upper limits of what this miraculous ingredient has to offer.

WHITE CHOCOLATE–CHARTREUSE
ICE CREAM

MAKES 2¼ QUARTS * PREP/COOK TIME: 25 MINUTES, PLUS CHILLING AND FREEZING

White chocolate is not really chocolate (shhhh!); it is a simple blend of cocoa butter, sugar, and milk solids. Its neutrality and richness is a perfect foil for something as herbaceous and haunting as Chartreuse liqueur. Chartreuse has been made by monks in France for nearly 300 years under a closely guarded recipe with some 130 ingredients, mainly flowers and herbs. It comes in green and yellow varieties; we prefer the green version for ice cream as it is slightly less sweet than the yellow and has a higher alcohol content, meaning less is required for maximum flavor and optimum freezing.

10 ounces white chocolate, finely chopped

12 extra-large egg yolks

4 cups heavy (whipping) cream

2 cups half-and-half

1 cup plus 2 tablespoons sugar

¼ cup Chartreuse, or more to taste

MAKE THE BASE

Put the white chocolate in a large heat-proof bowl and set aside.

In a small heat-proof bowl, whisk the egg yolks to combine. Set aside.

In a heavy-bottomed 2-quart saucepan over medium-low heat, combine the cream, half-and-half, and sugar. Heat the mixture, stirring occasionally with a heat-proof spatula to dissolve the sugar, until it is steamy and hot. Do not allow the mixture to boil.

When the liquid is hot, temper the egg yolks by pouring 1 cup of the hot liquid into the yolks in a slow, steady stream, whisking constantly. Immediately pour the tempered yolks into the pot, whisking constantly to combine. Scrape out the bowl that contained the egg yolks, using a heat-proof spatula.

Lower the heat under the pot slightly, and use the spatula to stir and scrape the bottom of the pot to keep the yolks from scrambling. Continue to gently cook the custard base, stirring constantly and adjusting the heat if necessary, until the base begins to thicken and evenly coats the spatula. This should take about 5 minutes.

Pour the custard over the chopped white chocolate and gently whisk until the chocolate is melted completely and combined into the custard.

Strain the mixture through a fine-mesh strainer into a 3-quart container. Stir the Chartreuse into the custard base, taste it, and adjust it to your liking with more Chartreuse, if needed. Cover the bowl with plastic wrap and refrigerate until thoroughly chilled, at least 2 hours or preferably overnight.

FREEZE

Place a 3-quart container with a tight-fitting lid in the freezer to chill. Freeze the chilled base according to your ice cream maker's instructions. Store the finished ice cream in the chilled container.

tip — Chartreuse is available in finer liquor stores; while expensive, a little goes a long way. Invest in a bottle and it should last the better part of a year even with regular sampling.

GIANDUJA
ICE CREAM

MAKES 2 QUARTS * PREP/COOK TIME: 1½ HOURS,
PLUS CHILLING, STEEPING, AND FREEZING

Gianduja (pronounced djan-DOO-yah) is difficult to say but very easy to eat. A true Italian classic, our recipe is adapted from a favorite gelateria that offers this creamy blend of deep chocolate and roasted hazelnuts. Italians have such an affinity for this flavor combination that they developed Nutella to meet the overwhelming demand. Hazelnut trees are nearly as plentiful as grapevines in northern and central Italy; in the early fall they play host to the truffle crop and by mid-autumn produce an abundance of nuts.

2½ cups whole raw hazelnuts

7 cups whole milk, divided

1 cup heavy (whipping) cream

5 ounces semisweet chocolate, chopped

3 ounces bittersweet chocolate, chopped

2¼ cups sugar, divided

Generous pinch kosher salt

12 extra-large egg yolks

Frangelico (optional)

PREP

Preheat the oven to 350°F.

Spread the hazelnuts in a single layer on a rimmed baking sheet and toast them, tossing occasionally and rotating the sheet to ensure even browning, 15 to 20 minutes. To test for doneness, carefully crack open a nut to gauge the interior color. It should be a deep toasted color but not burnt. If necessary, continue toasting, checking the nuts every 3 minutes until they are fully toasted.

When the hazelnuts are cool enough to handle, transfer them to a clean dishtowel. Gather the corners of the towel together and vigorously rub the nuts to remove as much of the skins as possible. Lift out the nuts, and set aside to cool completely.

MAKE THE BASE

Fill a large heat-proof bowl halfway with ice and nestle a smaller heat-proof bowl in the ice. Add 3 cups of milk and the heavy cream to the smaller bowl. Set aside.

In a double boiler or small stainless-steel bowl set over a pot of barely simmering water, melt the semisweet and bittersweet chocolate together. Set aside.

In a heavy-bottomed 4-quart pot, combine the remaining 4 cups of milk, 1 cup of sugar, and the salt. Heat the milk, stirring occasionally with a heat-proof spatula to dissolve the sugar and salt, until it is steamy and hot. Do not allow the mixture to boil. Remove the pot from the heat and set it aside.

Combine the hazelnuts and $\frac{1}{4}$ cup of sugar in a food processor and process them to a fine consistency, 1 to 2 minutes. Add the ground nuts to the scalded milk and stir to combine. Cover the pot with a tight-fitting lid and allow the mixture to steep for at least 30 minutes. Then return the pot to the stove and reheat the mixture over medium-low heat.

In a small heat-proof bowl, whisk the remaining 1 cup of sugar into the egg yolks to combine thoroughly.

When the hazelnut-milk mixture is hot, temper the egg yolks by pouring 1 cup of the hot liquid into the yolks in a slow, steady stream, whisking constantly. Immediately pour the tempered yolks into the pot, whisking constantly to combine. Scrape out the bowl that contained the egg yolks, using a heat-proof spatula.

Lower the heat under the pot slightly, and use the spatula to stir and scrape the bottom of the pot to keep the yolks from scrambling. Continue to gently cook the custard base, stirring constantly and adjusting the heat if necessary, until the base begins to thicken and evenly coats the spatula. This should take about 5 minutes.

Pour the custard into the bowl of melted chocolate. Mix together completely until smooth and uniform in color, then quickly add the custard base to the chilled milk and heavy cream, stirring everything together to stop the cooking process and combine.

Transfer the custard base to a 3-quart container with a tight-fitting lid and let the mixture steep in the refrigerator overnight.

Strain the custard base through a fine-mesh strainer, pressing on the nut solids to extract as much flavor as possible. Stir a bit of Frangelico (if using) into the strained base.

FREEZE

Place a 2-quart container with a tight-fitting lid in the freezer to chill. Freeze the ice cream according to your ice cream maker's instructions and store the finished ice cream in the chilled container.

STRACCIATELLA

MAKES 2 QUARTS * PREP/COOK TIME: 30 MINUTES, PLUS CHILLING AND FREEZING

Stracciatella (pronounced STRAH-chi-a-teh-la) is an Italian version of chocolate chip ice cream. Rather than chips, though, melted chocolate is drizzled in a fine stream into freshly spun ice cream and stirred to create thin bits of chocolate throughout. Its name comes from a simple Italian soup that has egg streamed into hot broth, creating ribbons of cooked egg throughout.

3 cups heavy (whipping) cream

8 extra-large egg yolks

1 ½ cups half-and-half

1 cup sugar

1 Madagascar vanilla bean

Generous pinch kosher salt

8 ounces bittersweet or semisweet chocolate, chopped

MAKE THE BASE

Fill a large heat-proof bowl halfway with ice. Nestle a smaller heat-proof bowl in the ice and place a fine-mesh strainer over it. Add the heavy cream to the smaller of the chilled bowls. Set aside.

In a small heat-proof bowl, whisk the egg yolks to combine. Set aside.

In a heavy-bottomed 4-quart pot over medium-low heat, combine the half-and-half, and sugar. Heat the mixture, stirring occasionally with a heat-proof spatula to dissolve the sugar, until it is steamy and hot. Do not allow the mixture to boil. Meanwhile, with a paring knife, split the vanilla bean lengthwise, scrape out the seeds, and add the pod and seeds to the warming liquid. >>

 tip We use vanilla ice cream here, but experiment with flavors; you can *"stracci"* just about anything. Some of our favorites are Coffee Ice Cream (page 45), Toasted Almond Ice Cream (page 43), and Toasted Coconut Ice Cream (page 93). Come to think of it, Peanut Butter Ice Cream (page 134) would be pretty good too! *Stracciatella* also makes a beautiful layer in a multi-flavored molded ice cream dessert.

When the liquid is hot, temper the egg yolks by pouring 1 cup of the hot liquid into the yolks in a slow, steady stream, whisking constantly. Immediately pour the tempered yolks into the pot, whisking constantly to combine. Scrape out the bowl that contained the egg yolks, using a heat-proof spatula.

Lower the heat under the pot slightly, and use the spatula to stir and scrape the bottom of the pot to keep the yolks from scrambling. Continue to gently cook the custard base, stirring constantly and adjusting the heat if necessary, until the base begins to thicken and evenly coats the spatula. This should take about 5 minutes.

Strain the custard into the chilled heavy cream. Do not scrape out the pot. Add the salt and stir the mixture to stop the cooking process and combine the custard and cream. Thoroughly chill the base over the ice, or cover the bowl with plastic wrap and refrigerate for at least 2 hours, or preferably overnight.

FREEZE

Place a 2-quart container with a tight-fitting lid in the freezer to chill. Freeze the ice cream base according to your ice cream maker's instructions.

MELT THE CHOCOLATE

When the ice cream is nearly ready, in a double boiler or small stainless-steel bowl set over a pan of barely simmering water, melt the chocolate, stirring occasionally, until it is smooth. Do not let any water get into the chocolate, and do not let it get too hot (see the Tip).

There are two ways to add the chocolate to the finished ice cream. You can pour the melted chocolate in a thin and steady stream into the ice cream freezer in the last moments of churning and let the machine do the mixing for you. Alternatively, you can drizzle it in as you are filling the chilled 2-quart container, using a fork to get thin strips of chocolate. Either drizzle some of the chocolate into the container and top with a thin layer of ice cream, repeating until all the chocolate and ice cream are used, or just drizzle the chocolate in, stirring as you go to break up the pieces more. Store the finished ice cream in the chilled container.

tip If your chocolate is too hot, it will not pour well, and you will end up with big pieces of chocolate in your ice cream rather than thin strips. Slightly cooled chocolate flows nicely and will allow you to achieve a thin drizzle much more easily.

DARK CHOCOLATE
ICE CREAM

MAKES 2 QUARTS * PREP/COOK TIME: 40 MINUTES, PLUS CHILLING AND FREEZING

Chocolate ice cream runs a close second to vanilla on the list of most requested flavors, and for good reason. It's simply delicious! This version, one of many we hold dear, has the addition of caramelized sugar for additional bitterness beyond the typical chocolate notes. The results are worth the extra effort.

6 cups whole milk

12 extra-large egg yolks

2⅜ cups sugar, divided

Generous pinch kosher salt

¼ teaspoon cream of tartar

3 tablespoons water

10½ ounces semisweet chocolate, chopped

½ cup plus 2 tablespoons unsweetened cocoa powder, sifted

MAKE THE BASE

Fill a large heat-proof bowl halfway with ice. Nestle a smaller heat-proof bowl in the ice and place a fine-mesh strainer over it. Set aside.

In a heavy-bottomed 2-quart saucepot over medium-low heat, heat the milk until steamy and hot. Do not allow the milk to boil. Remove the pot from the heat and set it aside in a warm place.

In an electric mixer fitted with the whisk attachment, beat the egg yolks, 2 cups of sugar, and the salt on high speed until the mixture is pale and fluffy, about 5 minutes. Set aside.

In a heavy-bottomed 4-quart pot, combine the remaining ⅜ cup of sugar and the cream of tartar. Stir in the water to moisten all the sugar. Brush down the sides of the pot with a wet pastry brush to remove any sugar particles, as this may cause the caramel to crystallize during cooking. >>

Place the pot over high heat and bring the mixture to a boil. Cook the sugar until it begins to caramelize, about 5 minutes, then lower the heat to medium and swirl the pot to keep the sugar from burning in hot spots. In 5 to 7 minutes, you should have an even, deep bronze, bubbling caramel.

Remove the pot from the heat. Stop the caramel from cooking by gradually and carefully adding the warm milk. Stand back! It will steam and bubble, and may splatter at first. Whisk the milk and caramel together and set aside.

In a double boiler or a large stainless-steel bowl set over a pot of barely simmering water, melt the chocolate. Slowly whisk the warm caramel into the melted chocolate. Pour the entire mixture back into the 4-quart pot and place the pot over medium-low heat.

When the liquid is hot, temper the egg yolks by slowly pouring the hot chocolate-caramel mixture into the egg yolks in a slow, steady stream, whisking constantly. Scrape out the pot to get all of the chocolate-caramel. Once thoroughly mixed, transfer the mixture back into the pot.

Over low heat, whisk the cocoa powder into the chocolate-caramel mixture. Remove any large lumps, but don't worry if it is not completely smooth. Gently heat the mixture until the cocoa powder has been absorbed, about 2 minutes.

Pour the ice cream base through the strainer into the smaller of the chilled bowls and press any solids through. Cover the bowl with plastic wrap and thoroughly chill in the refrigerator for at least 2 hours, or preferably overnight.

FREEZE

Place a 2-quart container with a tight-fitting lid in the freezer to chill. Freeze the chilled base according to your ice cream maker's instructions. Store the finished ice cream in the chilled 2-quart container.

MEXICAN CHOCOLATE
ICE CREAM WITH CHURROS

MAKES 1½ QUARTS ❋ PREP/COOK TIME: 45 MINUTES, PLUS CHILLING AND FREEZING

Mexican chocolate is famous for its versatility—its prominent grainy texture, sweetness level, and spicy cinnamon notes allow it to animate dishes ranging from savory mole to hot chocolate. There are several widely available brands of Mexican chocolate that make this recipe an anytime indulgence. Fry up a batch of cinnamon sugar–coated *churros,* then pair the hot, crispy dough sticks with this ice cream for a frosty take on hot chocolate.

FOR THE ICE CREAM

8½ ounces Mexican chocolate, such as Ibarra or Taza, chopped

4 cups heavy (whipping) cream

12 extra-large egg yolks

2½ cups half-and-half

1⅓ cups sugar

Generous pinch kosher salt

2 teaspoons brandy (optional)

FOR THE CHURROS

6 cups canola oil

½ cup water

½ cup whole milk

½ cup (1 stick) unsalted butter

½ cup sugar, divided

Generous pinch kosher salt

1 cup all-purpose flour

4 extra-large eggs

2 teaspoons ground cinnamon

PREP

In a double boiler or stainless-steel bowl set over a pot of barely simmering water, melt the chocolate. Set aside.

MAKE THE BASE

Fill a large heat-proof bowl halfway with ice. Nestle a smaller heat-proof bowl in the ice and place a fine-mesh strainer over it. Add the heavy cream to the smaller of the chilled bowls. Set aside.

In a small heat-proof bowl, whisk the egg yolks to combine. Set aside. >>

In a heavy-bottomed 4-quart pot over medium-low heat, combine the half-and-half, sugar, and salt. Heat the mixture, stirring occasionally with a heat-proof spatula to dissolve the sugar and salt, until it is steamy and hot. Do not allow the mixture to boil.

When the liquid is hot, temper the egg yolks by pouring 1 cup of the hot liquid into the yolks in a slow, steady stream, whisking constantly. Immediately pour the tempered yolks into the pot, whisking constantly to combine. Scrape out the bowl that contained the egg yolks, using a heat-proof spatula.

Lower the heat under the pot slightly, and use the spatula to stir and scrape the bottom of the pot to keep the yolks from scrambling. Continue to gently cook the custard base, stirring constantly and adjusting the heat if necessary, until the base begins to thicken and evenly coats the spatula. This should take about 5 minutes.

Slowly whisk the custard into the melted chocolate. Strain the chocolate mixture into the chilled heavy cream, stirring until the cream and custard are blended completely. Thoroughly chill the base over the ice, or cover the bowl with plastic wrap and refrigerate for at least 2 hours, or preferably overnight.

FREEZE

Place a 2-quart container with a tight-fitting lid in the freezer to chill. Freeze the chilled base according to your ice cream maker's instructions. Store the finished ice cream in the chilled 2-quart container.

MAKE THE CHURROS

Fill a heavy-bottomed 4-quart pot with the canola oil and clip a candy thermometer to the edge of the pot, submerged at least an inch deep in the oil. Make certain the thermometer does not touch the bottom of the pot. Heat the oil to 350°F.

In a small saucepan over medium-high heat, combine the water, milk, butter, ¼ cup of sugar, and the salt and bring it to a boil. Add the flour all at once, and stir to combine it with the liquid, using a wooden spoon. Lower the heat to medium and stir until no lumps of flour remain. Cook the dough, stirring occasionally, for 2 to 3 minutes to help evaporate some of the moisture. It should come together in a sticky mass with a thin layer of dough forming on the bottom of the pan.

Transfer the cooked dough to an electric mixer fitted with the paddle attachment. Beat the mixture on medium-high speed for 1 minute to cool it slightly. Crack the eggs into a 2-cup measuring cup and have them ready to add to the dough. Lower the mixer to medium speed and add the eggs, one at a time, beating the mixture until the eggs are fully incorporated. Stop the mixer and scrape down the sides of the bowl, then beat the mixture for another 30 seconds. Transfer the finished churro dough to a pastry bag lined with a star tip (see the Tip).

When the canola oil reaches 350°F, carefully pipe the dough into the hot oil in 6-inch lengths, separating each churro by trimming at the tip with a paring knife. Fry three or four churros at a time, being careful to not overcrowd the pot. Be sure to maintain the oil temperature at 350°F. Fry the dough until it is puffed and golden brown, 3 to 5 minutes. Transfer the finished churros with a slotted spoon to a paper towel–lined plate. Repeat the frying until all the dough has been used.

In a large bowl combine the cinnamon and remaining $\frac{1}{4}$ cup of sugar.

Toss the warm churros in the cinnamon-sugar until coated. Shake off any extra cinnamon-sugar and mound the churros on a serving platter.

tip A pastry bag is a reusable, cone-shaped canvas or silicone-lined bag used for filling cream puffs, applying icing to cakes, or, in this case, piping churros into hot oil. A variety of interchangeable metal tips can be inserted into the bag for different piped designs. We prefer a star tip when making churros as it creates ridges where the cinnamon sugar can adhere.

COOKIES AND CREMA

MAKES 2 QUARTS * PREP TIME: 5 MINUTES, PLUS FREEZING

How can you go wrong combining two delicious ingredients like freshly baked chocolate wafer cookies and rich *crema* ice cream? This worldwide favorite is fun and simple to make at home. Bake a tray of chocolate cookies, crush them to your liking, and swirl into a batch of churned ice cream. The flavor will intensify as it rests, so plan on making the blend-in either the morning of the day you plan to serve it or the day before.

15 Chocolate Wafer Cookies (page 217)

2 quarts Crema Ice Cream, just made (page 131)

PREP

Pulse the cookies in a food processor or crumble them by hand to break up into very small crumbs.

Once the ice cream is just finished freezing, fold in the cookie crumbs. Be generous: The ice cream should be well flecked with chocolate.

FREEZE

Transfer the ice cream to a chilled 2-quart container with a tight-fitting lid, and place it in the freezer for at least 3 hours, or preferably overnight.

CHOCOLATE-COVERED NUT
ICE CREAM

MAKES 2 QUARTS ❋ PREP TIME: 5 MINUTES, PLUS FREEZING

Chocolate-covered nuts stirred into Madagascar Vanilla Ice Cream (page 34) or Dark Chocolate Ice Cream (page 67) delivers two treats in one bite. Crunchy roasted nuts are encased in bittersweet chocolate, chopped finely, then swirled into a luscious classic ice cream base. How can it get better than this?

1 recipe Chocolate-Covered Nuts (page 212)

2 quarts Madagascar Vanilla Ice Cream (page 34) or Dark Chocolate Ice Cream (page 67), just made

PREP

Chop the chocolate-covered nuts by hand and place them in the freezer until ready to swirl into the ice cream.

Fold the chocolate-covered nuts into the ice cream.

FREEZE

Transfer the ice cream to a chilled 2-quart container with a tight-fitting lid, and place it in the freezer for at least 3 hours, or preferably overnight.

tip While you can go with any nuts you choose, we tend to use chocolate-covered almonds in this ice cream.

MALTED MILK CHOCOLATE
ICE CREAM

MAKES 2 QUARTS * PREP/COOK TIME: 30 MINUTES, PLUS FREEZING

Malted milk reminds us of our childhoods. Some of Anthony's earliest childhood memories are getting off the school bus to head home but instead ducking into the neighborhood corner store. More candy shop than grocery market, most loose sweets were 1¢ each, or 5¢ for the wrapped confections. Nestled there in between the Tootsie Rolls and Swedish Fish was a glorious mound of pea-size, candy-coated malted milk balls. A small paper sackful set you back 25¢ at most, and that was more than enough to share with friends.

9 ounces milk chocolate, chopped

4 cups heavy (whipping) cream

12 extra-large egg yolks

2½ cups half-and-half

1⅓ cups sugar

Generous pinch kosher salt

1 cup malted milk powder

PREP

In a double boiler or a stainless-steel bowl set over a pot of barely simmering water, melt the chocolate. Set aside.

MAKE THE BASE

Fill a large heat-proof bowl halfway with ice. Nestle a smaller heat-proof bowl in the ice and place a fine-mesh strainer over it. Add the heavy cream to the smaller of the chilled bowls. Set aside.

In a small heat-proof bowl, whisk the egg yolks to combine. Set aside.

In a heavy-bottomed 4-quart pot over medium-low heat, combine the half-and-half, sugar, the salt, and malted milk powder. Heat the mixture, whisking to dissolve the solids to make sure there are no lumps. Do not allow the mixture to boil.

74 PERFECTLY SIMPLE ICE CREAM

When the liquid is hot, temper the egg yolks by pouring 1 cup of the hot liquid into the yolks in a slow, steady stream, whisking constantly. Immediately pour the tempered yolks into the pot, whisking constantly to combine. Scrape out the bowl that contained the egg yolks, using a heat-proof spatula.

Lower the heat under the pot slightly, and use the spatula to stir and scrape the bottom of the pot to keep the yolks from scrambling. Continue to gently cook the custard base, stirring constantly and adjusting the heat if necessary, until the base begins to thicken and evenly coats the spatula. This should take about 5 minutes.

Slowly whisk the custard into the melted chocolate, stirring to combine thoroughly. Strain the chocolate mixture into the chilled heavy cream and stir so that it is completely blended. Thoroughly chill the base over the ice, or cover the bowl with plastic wrap and refrigerate for at least 2 hours, or preferably overnight.

FREEZE

Place a 2-quart container with a tight-fitting lid in the freezer to chill. Freeze the ice cream according to your ice cream maker's instructions. Store the finished ice cream in the chilled container.

BITTERSWEET CHOCOLATE
SHERBET

MAKES 2 QUARTS ✳ PREP/COOK TIME: 45 MINUTES, PLUS FREEZING

Can chocolate be refreshing? Yes! Think of how much you loved fudge pops as a kid. Now you can make your own and have it any time you like, not just when Mom says you can. This sherbet pairs well with so many flavors, from fruit to nuts, and makes a simple and elegant crispy meringue dessert with whipped cream and a few chocolate shavings. Check out the Crispy Meringue Boats (page 163).

8 ounces bittersweet chocolate, chopped

8 ounces semisweet chocolate, chopped

5¼ cups water, divided

¾ teaspoon powdered gelatin

1¼ to 1½ cups sugar

¾ cup unsweetened cocoa powder

½ cup heavy (whipping) cream

2 teaspoons pure vanilla extract

Generous pinch kosher salt

MAKE THE BASE

Combine the bittersweet and semisweet chocolate in a large stainless-steel bowl. Set aside.

Put ¼ cup of cold water in a small saucepan and sprinkle the gelatin over it. Set it aside for 5 to 10 minutes to bloom.

Meanwhile, in a heavy-bottomed 2-quart pot, bring the remaining 5 cups of water and 1¼ cups of sugar to a boil, stirring occasionally to dissolve the sugar. Reduce the heat to medium-low and slowly whisk in the cocoa powder. Increase the heat to high and boil the mixture for 2 minutes.

Pour the hot mixture over the chopped chocolate. Cover the bowl with plastic wrap and let it sit for 2 minutes. Then remove the plastic wrap and whisk the mixture until it is smooth. Let the mixture cool a bit, just until it is warm to the touch but not hot.

Place the saucepan of gelatin over low heat. Warm it just until all the gelatin is dissolved, then slowly whisk it into the chocolate mixture, being sure to mix everything well. Stir in the heavy cream, vanilla, and salt and mix well. Thoroughly chill the base over the ice, or cover the bowl with plastic wrap and refrigerate for at least 2 hours, or preferably overnight.

FREEZE

Place a 2-quart container with a tight-fitting lid in the freezer to chill. Before adding the sherbet

base to the ice cream machine, give it a stir and taste for sweetness, adding up to ¼ cup more sugar if desired. Freeze the sherbet according to your ice cream maker's instructions. Store the finished sherbet in the chilled container.

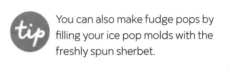

tip You can also make fudge pops by filling your ice pop molds with the freshly spun sherbet.

MOCHA
ICE CREAM

MAKES 2 QUARTS * PREP/COOK TIME: 45 MINUTES, PLUS FREEZING

Coffee and chocolate share similar flavor profiles, and when they are in balance they can be truly soul satisfying. Italian baristas have perfected hot chocolate with espresso; this is our entry for semisweet chocolate ice cream with a coffee kick. We steep whole beans in warm half-and-half, then cold-steep the finished base for extra extraction.

7½ ounces semisweet chocolate, chopped

1½ ounces bittersweet chocolate, chopped

4 cups heavy (whipping) cream

2½ cups half-and-half

1⅓ cups sugar

Generous pinch kosher salt

1 cup whole coffee beans

12 extra-large egg yolks

PREP

In a double boiler or a stainless-steel bowl set over a pot of barely simmering water, melt the chocolate. Set aside.

MAKE THE BASE

Fill a large heat-proof bowl halfway with ice. Nestle a smaller heat-proof bowl in the ice and place a fine-mesh strainer over it. Add the heavy cream to the smaller of the chilled bowls. Set aside.

In a heavy-bottomed 4-quart pot over medium-low heat, combine the half-and-half, sugar, and salt. Heat the mixture, stirring occasionally to dissolve the sugar and salt, until it is steamy and hot. Do not allow the mixture to boil. When the mixture is hot and the sugar and salt are dissolved, add the coffee beans, then remove the pot from the heat and allow the beans to steep in the liquid for 30 minutes.

In a small heat-proof bowl, whisk the egg yolks to combine. Temper the egg yolks by pouring 1 cup of the warm liquid into the yolks in a slow, steady stream, whisking constantly. Immediately pour the tempered yolks into the pot, whisking constantly to combine. Scrape out the bowl that contained the egg yolks, using a heat-proof spatula.

Set the pot over low heat, and use the spatula to stir and scrape the bottom of the pot to keep the yolks from scrambling. Continue to gently cook the custard base, stirring constantly and adjusting the heat if necessary, until the base begins to thicken and evenly coats the spatula. This should take about 5 minutes.

Whisk the custard into the melted chocolate until the custard and chocolate are well mixed. Strain the chocolate-custard mixture into the chilled heavy cream and stir so that it is completely blended. Thoroughly chill the base over the ice, or cover the bowl with plastic wrap and refrigerate for at least 2 hours, or preferably overnight. (If you want a stronger coffee flavor, pour the mixture directly into the heavy cream,

not through the fine-mesh strainer. Mix well, cover the bowl with plastic wrap, and refrigerate overnight. The next day, strain the mixture through the fine-mesh strainer before freezing. Either way, remove the coffee beans before freezing.)

FREEZE

Place a 2-quart container with a tight-fitting lid in the freezer to chill. Freeze the ice cream according to your ice cream maker's instructions. Store the finished ice cream in the chilled container.

tip Decaffeinated coffee beans contain the same flavor as regular beans, but they are processed to remove the stimulant. If you are planning on serving this ice cream to a large group, where some may have an aversion to caffeine, go with decaf; otherwise full-strength beans will suffice.

TARTUFO

Tartufo is the Italian word for truffle—the chocolate candy version, not the highly prized mushroom. The candy, of course, is its own kind of delicacy, and we have our own ode to those glorious black diamonds of winter: Two different ice creams, one inside the other, shaped into a giant truffle and rolled in cocoa powder, crushed wafer cookies, or a variety of other jackets.

1 quart Coffee Ice Cream (page 45)

1 quart Gianduja Ice Cream (page 62)

1 cup unsweetened cocoa powder, sifted, or 1 cup crushed Chocolate Wafer Cookies (page 217)

Line a baking sheet with parchment paper or a silicone baking mat. Make sure to use a baking sheet that will fit in your freezer.

Using an ice cream scoop, portion eight scoops of one of the ice creams, flattening the bottom so it is flush with the edge of the scoop, on the parchment paper, flat-side down. This will be the outer shell of the tartufo. Using a smaller scoop, portion four round (not flattened) scoops of the other ice cream onto the parchment paper; this will be the interior layer of the tartufo.

Cover the baking sheet with plastic wrap and transfer it to the freezer to allow the ice cream to firm up, about 2 hours.

Remove the baking sheet from the freezer and quickly build the tartufo. Make a hole in the flat side of two of the large scoops. Place a round scoop of the second flavor in one of the holes and cover it with the hole in the other large scoop. Press the two large halves around the smaller scoop. Working quickly, shape the ice cream into a rough ball and place it back on the parchment paper. Repeat for the three remaining tartufi. Cover the baking sheet with plastic wrap and return it to the freezer for 3 hours, or preferably overnight.

When ready to serve, place the cocoa powder or cookie crumbs in a medium bowl and roll each tartufo in the coating. Evenly coat the tartufi so no ice cream is visible and it resembles a large black truffle. Serve in an attractive sundae coupe.

tip You can pair any two ice creams you like to make a tartufo. Coffee and gianduja just happens to be one of our favorite combos.

CHOCOLATE-ORANGE
SHERBET

MAKES 1¼ QUARTS ❋ PREP/COOK TIME: 30 MINUTES, PLUS FREEZING

Chocolate and citrus are a winning combination in almost any form. Since there is not an abundance of ingredients in this recipe, opt for high-quality bittersweet chocolate, containing at least 70 percent cacao, and freshly squeezed organic orange juice. If you have access to blood oranges in winter, they can be freely substituted for a more robust and complex sherbet.

2½ cups water

1 cup plus 2 tablespoons sugar

Generous pinch kosher salt

14 ounces bittersweet chocolate, chopped

3⅓ cups freshly squeezed orange juice, pulp strained out

1 tablespoon Grand Marnier or orange liqueur (optional)

MAKE THE BASE

In a heavy-bottomed 2-quart pot over medium heat, combine the water, sugar, and salt, stirring occasionally to dissolve the sugar. Once the syrup comes to a boil and the sugar is dissolved, remove the pot from the heat and set it aside to cool slightly, about 5 minutes.

In a double boiler or a stainless-steel bowl set over a pot of barely simmering water, slowly melt the chocolate. Once it is melted, whisk it into the syrup.

Stir the orange juice and Grand Marnier (if using) into the chocolate syrup.

FREEZE

Place a 2-quart container with a tight-fitting lid in the freezer to chill. Freeze the sherbet base according to your ice cream maker's instructions. Store the finished sherbet in the chilled 2-quart container.

 A double boiler is a foolproof method to warm ingredients utilizing indirect heat. Alternatively, a heat-proof bowl can be set over a small pot of simmering water to protect the ingredients from scalding or burning.

fruity

The bounty of seasonal fruits can easily be transformed into delicious frozen treats, making this chapter one you will return to repeatedly. The fruit supply crests in the summer, with berries and stone fruit and melons, as well as fresh herbs. Fall brings wine and table grapes, pears, and huckleberries, followed by the cavalcade of winter citrus. Cherries and apricots in the springtime are a welcome sight after a long, sparse winter. The cycle repeats when the first strawberries appear, which are, of course, ideal for making ice creams, sherbets, and sauces.

CREAMY LIME
SHERBET

MAKES 1½ QUARTS * PREP TIME: 2 HOURS, 10 MINUTES, PLUS CHILLING AND FREEZING

When the price of limes drops to five for a buck, we take full advantage and start juicing in earnest. Lime juice is the brightest and most acidic citrus juice we work with, so it needs to be diluted and heavily sweetened. We prefer the juicy Bearss lime, developed in California, with its aromatic zest and floral yet spicy notes. They are marketed as Persian limes around the rest of the country. For the best possible juice extraction, choose limes that have begun to turn yellow, are unblemished, and feel heavy for their size.

2 cups sugar, plus more to taste

⅛ teaspoon kosher salt

3 limes, for zest

2⅔ cups freshly squeezed lime juice

1¼ cups water, plus more to taste

1 cup whole milk, plus more to taste

MAKE THE BASE

Combine the sugar and salt in a small bowl and Microplane the lime zest directly onto the sugar to capture its essential oils. Add the lime juice, water, and milk and stir until the sugar and salt are dissolved completely. Taste and adjust, if needed, with a few more tablespoons each of water, milk, or sugar. The sherbet mixture should be bright, citrusy, sweet, and not too sour or acidic.

Cover the bowl with plastic wrap and chill the sherbet base thoroughly in the refrigerator for at least 2 hours, or preferably overnight.

FREEZE

Place a 2-quart container with a tight-fitting lid in the freezer to chill. Freeze the sherbet according to your ice cream maker's instructions. Store the finished sherbet in the chilled container.

 tip A Microplane is a handy wand-shaped tool that makes quick work of finely zesting citrus or grating chocolate, as well as savory items, such as cheese or spices.

PASSION FRUIT
ICE CREAM

MAKES 2 QUARTS ✴ PREP/COOK TIME: 30 MINUTES, PLUS CHILLING AND FREEZING

In the winter months, when the fruit crop is scarce and the days short and grey, we long for something other than citrus or chocolate for dessert. We turn to passion fruit for an intense, floral, puckery respite. The fruit of a climbing vine native to Brazil, it is now being grown in temperate zones across California. Fortunately, the frozen pulp is available and quite affordable through online retailers like Amazon. We prefer a brand such as Boiron, which offers purées "not from concentrate," since heat would damage the brightness and acidity.

4 cups heavy (whipping) cream

12 extra-large egg yolks

2½ cups half-and-half

1⅓ cups sugar, plus more to taste

Generous pinch kosher salt

½ cup passion fruit purée

Few drops freshly squeezed orange juice
    or lemon juice (optional)

MAKE THE BASE

Fill a large heat-proof bowl halfway with ice. Nestle a smaller heat-proof bowl in the ice and place a fine-mesh strainer over it. Add the heavy cream to the smaller of the chilled bowls. Set aside.

In a small heat-proof bowl, whisk the egg yolks to combine. Set aside.

In a heavy-bottomed 4-quart pot over medium heat, combine the half-and-half, sugar, and salt. Heat the mixture, stirring occasionally with a heat-proof spatula to dissolve the sugar and salt, until it is steamy and hot. Do not allow the mixture to boil.

When the liquid is hot, temper the egg yolks by pouring 1 cup of the hot liquid into the yolks in a slow, steady stream, whisking constantly. Immediately pour the tempered yolks into the pot, whisking constantly to combine. Scrape out the bowl that contained the egg yolks, using a heat-proof spatula.

Lower the heat under the pot slightly, and use the spatula to stir and scrape the bottom of the pot to keep the yolks from scrambling. Continue to gently cook the custard base, stirring constantly and adjusting the >>

heat if necessary, until the base begins to thicken and evenly coats the spatula. This should take about 5 minutes.

Strain the custard into the chilled heavy cream. Do not scrape out the pot. Stir the mixture to stop the cooking process and to combine the custard and cream.

Stir in the passion fruit purée and orange juice (if using) until well mixed. Taste the mixture and adjust with more sugar or orange juice if needed. Thoroughly chill the base over the ice, or cover the bowl with plastic wrap and refrigerate for at least 2 hours, or preferably overnight.

FREEZE

Place a 2-quart container with a tight-fitting lid in the freezer to chill. Freeze the ice cream according to your ice cream maker's instructions. Store the finished ice cream in the chilled container.

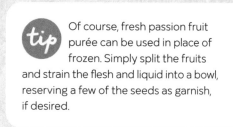

tip Of course, fresh passion fruit purée can be used in place of frozen. Simply split the fruits and strain the flesh and liquid into a bowl, reserving a few of the seeds as garnish, if desired.

PINEAPPLE
SHERBET

MAKES 1 QUART ✳ PREP TIME: 20 MINUTES, PLUS CHILLING AND FREEZING

Tropical flavors, in all their exotic and complex glory, make outstanding frozen desserts thanks to their inherent sweetness and vibrant flesh. Ripe pineapples are incredibly fragrant, with sweet, floral notes that translate to everything from cocktails to candied fruit. Pineapples ripen only slightly after harvesting, so be highly selective when choosing the fruit (see the Tip).

2 pineapples, peeled, cored, and cut into chunks

¾ cup sugar

Generous pinch kosher salt

1 tablespoon Kirschwasser or rum (optional)

 To pick out a nice ripe pineapple, look for a golden color all around. Use your nose; it should smell, well, like a pineapple, being both fragrant and sweet. Choose a leaf from the center of the fruit and give it a tug, straight up. If it's ripe, the leaf should come out easily. Congratulations, you've chosen a good pineapple!

MAKE THE BASE

Purée the pineapple in a food processor until smooth. Pass the fruit pulp through a medium-mesh strainer into a large bowl, pressing through as much juice and pulp as possible. There should be about 3 cups of purée.

Whisk in the sugar, salt, and Kirschwasser (if using). Continue stirring until the sugar is completely dissolved. Taste and adjust the sherbet base as needed. Cover the bowl with plastic wrap and chill the sherbet base thoroughly in the refrigerator for at least 2 hours, or preferably overnight.

FREEZE

Place a 1- to 2-quart container with a tight-fitting lid in the freezer to chill. Freeze the sherbet according to your ice cream maker's instructions. Store the finished sherbet in the chilled container.

TANGERINE
SHERBET

MAKES 2 QUARTS * PREP/COOK TIME: 45 MINUTES, PLUS CHILLING AND FREEZING

The start of the New Year marks the beginning of the glorious citrus season. One of the highlights is the arrival of the versatile and delicious tangerine. Tangerines can be eaten out of hand, tossed in a salad, candied, juiced, or made into sherbet. The flavor ranges from deep and rich to bright and tangy. This recipe will be a staple in your pantry all season long; select flavorful, high-acid tangerines for this sherbet.

7 cups freshly squeezed tangerine juice, pulp and seeds strained (from about 40 tangerines), divided

1 to 1½ cups sugar

Zest of 2 tangerines

Orange liqueur, such as Cointreau or Grand Marnier (optional)

MAKE THE BASE

In a small pot over medium heat, combine 1 cup of juice, 1 cup of sugar, and the zest. Heat, stirring occasionally, until the sugar is dissolved. Pour the hot liquid into a bowl with the remaining 6 cups of tangerine juice and mix well. Cover the bowl with plastic wrap and chill the sherbet base thoroughly in the refrigerator for at least 2 hours, or preferably overnight.

Before adding the sherbet base to the ice cream machine, give it a stir and taste for sweetness. If necessary, adjust the sweetness by adding up to ½ cup more remaining sugar, then stir in a splash of Cointreau (if using).

FREEZE

Place a 2-quart container with a tight-fitting lid in the freezer to chill. Freeze the sherbet according to your ice cream maker's instructions. Store the finished sherbet in the chilled container.

STRAWBERRY
SHERBET

MAKES 2 QUARTS * PREP TIME: 15 MINUTES, PLUS CHILLING AND FREEZING

We have the French to thank for cultivating the strawberry. It was they who collected the wild strawberries of the forest and transplanted them into their gardens. There are 103 different species and subspecies. Some of the more readily available varieties are Albion, Chandler, Quinault, and Seascape. All have different qualities, so when selecting, taste, taste, and taste some more!

4 (1-pint) baskets ripe strawberries

1 to 1½ cups sugar

Few drops Kirschwasser or framboise (optional)

tip Strawberries are cheapest and best by mid-summer, so purchase plenty and freeze your purée to use later. Look for fully ripe strawberries that are red all the way to the stem (although some varieties have a distinctive white shoulder). Turn the basket over to peek at the bottom to see if any are unripe or, worse, rotten.

PREP

Wash, dry, and hull the strawberries. Purée the berries in a blender or food processor until smooth, then pass half of the purée through a fine-mesh strainer. Add the strained purée back to the remaining seeded portion. (Leaving some seeds in the purée adds not only flavor, but a nice texture as well.)

MAKE THE BASE

Transfer the purée to a small bowl and add 1 cup of sugar. Stir until the sugar is fully dissolved. Cover the bowl with plastic wrap and chill the sherbet base thoroughly in the refrigerator for at least 2 hours, or preferably overnight.

Give the chilled sherbet base a stir and taste it for sweetness. Adjust by adding up to ½ cup more sugar. Stir in the Kirschwasser (if using).

FREEZE

Place a 2-quart container with a tight-fitting lid in the freezer to chill. Freeze the sherbet according to your ice cream maker's instructions. Store the finished sherbet in the chilled container.

CANDIED KUMQUAT
ICE CREAM

MAKES 2 QUARTS * PREP/COOK TIME: 30 MINUTES, PLUS CHILLING AND FREEZING

The bounty of winter citrus reaches its peak when tiny sour kumquats reach the market. Some eat them raw, out of hand, seeds and all, for a vitamin C explosion. We prefer to lightly candy them in syrup, then blend them into ice cream for Ice Cream Sundaes (page 122) or Crispy Meringue Boats (page 163). The syrup is delicious in cocktails and can be reserved for future candying projects. Candied kumquats keep indefinitely in the refrigerator but they are so tasty they won't last long.

1 cup water

3⅓ cups sugar, divided

2 cups sliced kumquats, seeds removed

4 cups heavy (whipping) cream

12 extra-large egg yolks

2½ cups half-and-half

Generous pinch kosher salt

1 Madagascar vanilla bean

PREP

In a small saucepan over high heat, combine the water and 2 cups of sugar, stirring to dissolve the sugar. Bring the water to a boil. Lower the heat to a simmer and add the kumquats. Simmer for 1 to 2 minutes, then remove the pan from the heat, cover the pan, and set aside to cool.

MAKE THE BASE

Fill a large heat-proof bowl halfway with ice. Nestle a smaller heat-proof bowl in the ice and place a fine-mesh strainer over it. Add the heavy cream to the smaller of the chilled bowls. Set aside.

In a small heat-proof bowl, whisk the egg yolks to combine. Set aside.

In a heavy-bottomed 4-quart pot over medium-low heat, combine the half-and-half, the remaining 1⅓ cups of sugar, and the salt, stirring occasionally with a heat-proof spatula to dissolve the sugar and salt, until it is steamy and hot. Do not allow the mixture to boil. Meanwhile, with a paring knife, split the vanilla bean lengthwise, scrape out the seeds, and add the pod and seeds to the warming liquid. >>

When the liquid in the pot is hot, temper the egg yolks by pouring 1 cup of the hot liquid into the yolks in a slow, steady stream, whisking constantly. Immediately pour the tempered yolks into the pot, whisking constantly to combine. Scrape out the bowl that contained the egg yolks, using a heat-proof spatula.

Lower the heat under the pot slightly, and use the spatula to stir and scrape the bottom of the pot to keep the yolks from scrambling. Continue to gently cook the custard base, stirring constantly and adjusting the heat if necessary, until the base begins to thicken and evenly coats the spatula. This should take about 5 minutes.

Strain the custard into the chilled heavy cream. Do not scrape out the saucepot. Stir the mixture to stop the cooking process and to combine the custard and cream. If desired, add the strained vanilla pod to the liquid. Thoroughly chill the mixture over the ice or cover the bowl with plastic wrap and refrigerate for at least 2 hours, or preferably overnight.

FREEZE

Place a 2-quart container with a tight-fitting lid in the freezer to chill. Remove the vanilla pod (if still in the base), and freeze the ice cream according to your ice cream maker's instructions.

ADD THE KUMQUATS

Drain the kumquats from the syrup and roughly chop the fruit. Fold the candied fruit into the just-frozen ice cream. Store the finished ice cream in the chilled container.

TOASTED COCONUT
ICE CREAM

MAKES 2 QUARTS * PREP/COOK TIME: 1½ HOURS, PLUS CHILLING AND FREEZING

If you love coconut flavor and you desire a richer, denser dessert than the Toasted Coconut Ice Milk (page 50), try this ice cream instead. The same principles are in play here: Perfectly toasted, shredded coconut lends its heady aroma to creamy custard. It pairs wonderfully well with icy sherbets and flaky granitas of the same flavor profile.

2 cups shredded coconut

2½ cups half-and-half

1⅓ cups sugar

Generous pinch kosher salt

4 cups heavy (whipping) cream

12 extra-large egg yolks

2 teaspoons rum (optional)

PREP

Preheat the oven to 325°F.

Line a baking sheet with parchment paper or a silicone baking mat, and spread the shredded coconut on it in a single layer. Toast the coconut, stirring occasionally, for 5 to 7 minutes.

In a heavy-bottomed 4-quart pot over medium-low heat, combine the half-and-half, toasted coconut, sugar, and salt, stirring occasionally with a heat-proof spatula to dissolve the sugar and salt. Do not allow the mixture to boil. When the sugar is dissolved and the half-and-half is hot, remove the pot from the heat, cover it, and set it aside for 1 hour to steep the coconut.

MAKE THE BASE

Fill a large heat-proof bowl halfway with ice. Nestle a smaller heat-proof bowl in the ice and place a fine-mesh strainer over it. Add the heavy cream to the smaller of the chilled bowls. Set aside.

In a small heat-proof bowl, whisk the egg yolks to combine. Set aside. >>

Return the pot with the coconut to the stove and rewarm over medium-low heat. When the mixture is hot, temper the egg yolks by pouring 1 cup of the hot liquid into the yolks in a slow, steady stream, whisking constantly. Immediately pour the tempered yolks into the pot, whisking constantly to combine. Scrape out the bowl that contained the egg yolks, using a heat-proof spatula.

Lower the heat under the pot slightly, and use the spatula to stir and scrape the bottom of the pot to keep the yolks from scrambling. Continue to gently cook the custard base, stirring constantly and adjusting the heat if necessary, until the base begins to thicken and evenly coats the spatula. This should take about 5 minutes.

Strain the custard into the chilled heavy cream. Do not scrape out the pot. Stir the mixture to stop the cooking and to combine the custard and cream. Use the back of a spoon or a spatula to press on the coconut solids to extract as much liquid and flavor as possible. Stir in the rum (if using). Thoroughly chill the mixture over the ice, or cover the bowl with plastic wrap and refrigerate for at least 2 hours, or preferably overnight.

FREEZE

Place a 2-quart container with a tight-fitting lid in the freezer to chill. Freeze the ice cream according to your ice cream maker's instructions. Store the finished ice cream in the chilled container.

PEAR
SHERBET

MAKES 2 QUARTS ✳ PREP/COOK TIME: 45 MINUTES, PLUS CHILLING AND FREEZING

There are over 3,000 cultivars of the pear, ranging from crisp and bright, to soft and juicy. The firmer varieties are well suited for baking, poaching, and eating out of hand . . . perhaps with a nice piece of cheese. The softer varieties produce a lovely, creamy sherbet.

6 pounds very ripe pears

½ cup water

1 to 1½ cups sugar

Juice of 1 lemon, divided

PREP

Peel and core the pears and cut them into medium-size pieces. Put them in a heavy-bottomed 4-quart pot and add the water. Cover the pot and cook the pears over medium heat, stirring occasionally, until they are heated through, about 10 minutes. This will help keep the pears from turning brown, as they tend to oxidize quickly.

Transfer the contents of the pot to a blender or food processor and purée them. Strain the purée through a fine-mesh strainer into a bowl to collect any firmer pieces of fruit. You should have about 4 cups of purée.

MAKE THE BASE

Add 1 cup of sugar and half of the lemon juice to the bowl. Stir until the sugar is dissolved. Cover the bowl with plastic wrap and chill the mixture thoroughly in the refrigerator for at least 2 hours, or preferably overnight.

Give the chilled sherbet base a stir and taste it for sweetness. If necessary, adjust by adding up to ½ cup more sugar and the remaining lemon juice, stirring to dissolve the sugar.

FREEZE

Place a 2-quart container with a tight-fitting lid in the freezer to chill. Freeze the sherbet according to your ice cream maker's instructions. Store the finished sherbet in the chilled container.

 Pears are picked when they are mature and firm but not ripe, then allowed to ripen in storage. A ripe pear will yield to slight pressure at the top next to the stem. Refrigerate ripe pears and use within a few days.

PEACH
SHERBET

MAKES 2 QUARTS ✳ PREP/COOK TIME: 45 MINUTES, PLUS CHILLING AND FREEZING

It is a glorious day when the season's first peaches arrive at the farmers' market. Anticipating that first bite, then leaning over the kitchen sink, slurping and dripping. . . . Peaches fit nicely into a full range of preparations, both savory and sweet. This simple sherbet is the closest thing to eating a fresh peach. Peaches tend to oxidize quickly, so we find that a brief cooking keeps the flesh from becoming brown.

3⅓ to 4 pounds ripe peaches

¼ cup water

1 to 1½ cups sugar

1 teaspoon freshly squeezed lemon juice

PREP

Peel and pit the peaches and cut them into medium-size pieces. Put them in a heavy-bottomed 4-quart pot and add the water. Cover the pot and cook the peaches over medium heat, stirring occasionally, until they are heated through, about 10 minutes. This will help keep the peaches from turning brown, as they tend to oxidize quickly.

Transfer the contents of the pot to a blender or food processor and purée them. Strain the purée through a medium-mesh strainer into a bowl to collect any skin bits or unwanted firmer pieces. You should have about 6 cups of purée.

MAKE THE BASE

Add 1 cup of sugar and the lemon juice and stir until the sugar is dissolved. Cover the bowl with plastic wrap and chill the sherbet base thoroughly in the refrigerator for at least 2 hours, or preferably overnight.

FREEZE

Place a 2-quart container with a tight-fitting lid in the freezer to chill.

Give the chilled sherbet base a stir and taste it for sweetness. If necessary, add up to $\frac{1}{2}$ cup more sugar, stirring to dissolve the sugar. Freeze the sherbet according to your ice cream maker's instructions. Store the finished sherbet in the chilled container.

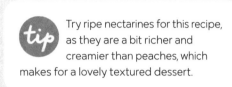

Try ripe nectarines for this recipe, as they are a bit richer and creamier than peaches, which makes for a lovely textured dessert.

BLOOD ORANGE
GRANITA

YIELD: ABOUT 4 CUPS ✳ PREP TIME: 10 MINUTES, PLUS FREEZING

Two of the most popular varietals of blood oranges grown in California are the Tarocco and the Moro. The fruits are interchangeable and equally good. The Tarocco has a lighter and more variegated flesh and is sweet, and the Moro is very dark throughout and tends to be more acidic.

1⅓ cups freshly squeezed blood orange juice, pulp and seeds strained (from about 6 blood oranges)

½ cup water

3 tablespoons sugar

Generous pinch kosher salt

Few drops orange liqueur, such as Cointreau or Grand Marnier (optional)

 tip A few drops of orange liqueur will give the magenta-colored, raspberry-esque juice of blood oranges a greater citrus balance. Be careful not to overdo it, though, as alcohol does not freeze.

PREP

Place an 8-by-12-inch glass or metal baking pan in the freezer to chill. The pan should rest flat on an easily accessible spot.

MAKE THE BASE

In a small bowl, stir together the blood orange juice, water, sugar, and salt until the sugar and salt are dissolved. Stir in the Grand Marnier (if using). Taste the mixture; it should be sweet but quite bright and acidic.

FREEZE

Remove the chilled baking pan from the freezer and pour in the liquid. Return the pan to the freezer. After 30 minutes, use a fork to stir the granita from the outside in, stirring any ice crystals back into the liquid. Return the pan to the freezer. Repeat this step every 30 minutes for at least 3 hours, or until the entire mixture has frozen and has a uniformly light, "dry," crystalline, icy texture. When the granita has reached this stage, cover it tightly with plastic wrap until you are ready to serve.

LEMON
ICE CREAM

MAKES 2 QUARTS * PREP/COOK TIME: 1 HOUR, 30 MINUTES, PLUS CHILLING AND FREEZING

You do not often see citrus-flavored ice creams as they are generally reserved for their icier sherbet and granita cousins. But we love citrus ice creams. If the citric acid present in lemon juice is properly tamed, what you get is the essence of the fruit. Combine the bracing refreshment of lemon juice with the bite of its zest, then add sweet cream for a headlining dessert.

1⅓ cups sugar, or more to taste

6 lemons, for zest

2½ cups half-and-half

4 cups heavy (whipping) cream

12 extra-large egg yolks

1 cup freshly squeezed lemon juice, divided

Generous pinch kosher salt

PREP

Put the sugar in a large bowl. Zest the lemons directly onto the sugar.

In a heavy-bottomed 4-quart pot over medium low heat, combine the half-and-half, sugar, and zest. Heat the mixture, stirring occasionally with a heat-proof spatula to dissolve the sugar, until it is steamy and hot. Do not allow the mixture to boil. Remove the pot from the heat, cover it, and set it aside for 1 hour to steep.

MAKE THE BASE

Fill a large heat-proof bowl halfway with ice. Nestle a smaller heat-proof bowl in the ice and place a fine-mesh strainer over it. Add the heavy cream to the smaller of the chilled bowls. Set aside.

Place the egg yolks in a small heat-proof bowl, and whisk them to combine. Set aside.

Return the pot to the stove and rewarm it over medium-low heat. When the liquid is hot, temper the egg yolks by pouring 1 cup of the hot liquid into the yolks in a slow, steady stream, whisking constantly. Immediately pour the tempered yolks into the pot, whisking constantly to combine. Scrape out the bowl that contained the egg yolks, using a heat-proof spatula.

Lower the heat under the pot slightly, and use the spatula to stir and scrape the bottom of the pot to keep the yolks from scrambling. Continue to gently cook the custard base, stirring constantly and adjusting the heat if necessary, until the base begins to thicken and evenly coats the spatula. This should take about 5 minutes.

Strain the custard into the chilled heavy cream. Do not scrape out the pot. Stir the mixture to stop the cooking process and to combine the custard and cream. Stir in $\frac{3}{4}$ cup of lemon juice and the salt. Taste the base and adjust it, if needed, with some of the remaining $\frac{1}{4}$ cup of lemon juice and more sugar. Thoroughly chill the ice cream base over the ice or cover the bowl with plastic wrap and refrigerate for at least 2 hours, or preferably overnight.

FREEZE

Place a 2-quart container with a tight-fitting lid in the freezer to chill. Freeze the ice cream according to your ice cream maker's instructions. Store the finished ice cream in the chilled container.

APRICOT
SHERBET

MAKES 2 QUARTS * PREP/COOK TIME: 30 MINUTES, PLUS CHILLING AND FREEZING

Apricots are thought to have originated in China, while some sources point to Armenia and India. Almost all US production of apricots comes from California, with several varieties to choose from. Our favorites include the early Poppy, Robada, and Castlebrite. The end of the season brings the stars of the show, the Blenheims and Royal Blenheims (one of the most divine fruits of the year). The low moisture content of apricots produces a creamy texture in this sherbet, even though the recipe lacks dairy.

4 pounds apricots

1 cup water

1 to 1½ cups sugar

PREP

Halve the apricots and keep two of the pits. Crack the two pits using a mallet or hammer to release the interior kernel to cook along with the fruit. Put all the apricots and the two kernels in a heavy-bottomed 4-quart pot and add the water. Cover the pot and cook the apricots over low heat, stirring occasionally to prevent the fruit from sticking and scorching, until the fruit is tender, about 10 minutes. Remove the apricot kernels and discard.

Transfer the contents of the pot to a blender or food processor and purée. Strain the purée through a medium-mesh strainer into a bowl to collect any bits of skin or unwanted firmer pieces. You should have about 6 cups of purée.

MAKE THE BASE

Add 1 cup of sugar and stir until the sugar is dissolved. Cover the bowl with plastic wrap and chill the mixture thoroughly in the refrigerator for at least 2 hours, or preferably overnight.

FREEZE

Place a 2-quart container with a tight-fitting lid in the freezer to chill.

Give the chilled sherbet base a stir and taste it for sweetness. If needed, adjust it by adding up to $\frac{1}{2}$ cup more sugar, stirring to dissolve the sugar. Freeze the sherbet according to your ice cream maker's instructions. Store the finished sherbet in the chilled container.

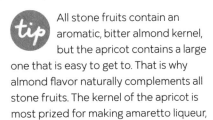

All stone fruits contain an aromatic, bitter almond kernel, but the apricot contains a large one that is easy to get to. That is why almond flavor naturally complements all stone fruits. The kernel of the apricot is most prized for making amaretto liqueur, amaretti cookies, and almond paste.

PLUM
ICE CREAM

MAKES 2 QUARTS ❋ PREP/COOK TIME: 45 MINUTES, PLUS CHILLING AND FREEZING

A stunning variety of plums grow all over the world. They range from small, tart, and astringent to large, sweet, and juicy. California is particularly suited to plum cultivation and provides us with varieties such as Greengage, Satsuma, Elephant Heart, Laroda, Howard Miracle, Emerald Beaut, and—our favorite—the divine Santa Rosa. The bright, tart skin and sweet, juicy flesh contribute to the full flavor of this ice cream.

6 to 8 ripe plums

¼ cup water

1¼ to 1½ cups sugar, divided

1½ cups heavy (whipping) cream

4 extra-large egg yolks

¾ cup half-and-half

Generous pinch salt

PREP

Halve and pit the plums. Cut the plum halves into rough pieces and transfer them to a heavy-bottomed 4-quart pot. Add the water, cover the pot, and heat the plums over medium heat, stirring occasionally to prevent the fruit from scorching. Cook until the fruit is tender and falling apart, about 10 minutes.

Transfer the contents of the pot to a blender or food processor and purée the plums. Strain the purée through a medium-mesh strainer into a bowl so only small bits of the flavorful skin remain in the purée. You should have about 4 cups of purée.

Add $\frac{3}{4}$ cup of sugar to the purée and stir until the sugar is dissolved. Cover the bowl with plastic wrap and chill the mixture thoroughly in the refrigerator for at least 2 hours, or preferably overnight.

MAKE THE BASE

Fill a large heat-proof bowl halfway with ice. Nestle a smaller heat-proof bowl in the ice and place a fine-mesh strainer over it. Add the heavy cream to the smaller of the chilled bowls. Set aside.

In a small heat-proof bowl, whisk the egg yolks to combine. Set aside.

In a heavy-bottomed 2-quart saucepot over medium heat, combine the half-and-half and $\frac{1}{2}$ cup of sugar. Heat the mixture, stirring occasionally with a heat-proof spatula to dissolve the sugar, until it is steamy and quite hot. Do not allow the mixture to boil.

When the liquid is hot, temper the egg yolks by pouring about $\frac{1}{2}$ cup of the hot liquid into the yolks in a slow, steady stream, whisking constantly. Immediately pour the tempered yolks into the pot, whisking constantly to combine. Scrape out the bowl that contained the egg yolks, using a heat-proof spatula.

Lower the heat under the pot slightly, and use the spatula to stir and scrape the bottom of the pot to keep the yolks from scrambling. Continue to gently cook the custard base, stirring constantly and adjusting the heat if necessary, until the base begins to thicken and evenly coats the spatula. This should take about 5 minutes.

Strain the base into the chilled heavy cream. Do not scrape out the pot. Stir the mixture to stop the cooking process and to combine the custard and cream. Thoroughly chill the base over the ice, or cover the bowl with plastic wrap and refrigerate for at least 2 hours, or preferably overnight.

Combine the chilled purée and ice cream base in a 1-to-1 ratio. In other words, if you have 4 cups of purée, add 4 cups of ice cream base. Mix well and taste. If needed, adjust the flavor with up to $\frac{1}{4}$ cup more sugar.

FREEZE

Place a 2-quart container with a tight-fitting lid in the freezer to chill. Freeze the ice cream according to your ice cream maker's instructions. Store the finished ice cream in the chilled container.

 For plum sherbet, simply make the sweetened plum purée, chill it, and spin in your ice cream machine. Plum sherbet is rich and intense. It's delicious either along-side a scoop of vanilla ice cream or other neutral flavor, or with a dollop of Perfectly Whipped Cream (page 207) and a gingersnap.

CHAPTER SIX

nostalgic

By definition, nostalgia is a sentimental longing or affection for the past, typically for a period or place with happy personal associations. And so what follows is a collection of recipes that has delivered exactly that: many, many happy personal associations with the past. We can't help the fact that so many of our favorite memories, special occasions, holidays, family celebrations, and simply being a kid are attached to eating ice cream.

ROCKY ROAD
ICE CREAM

MAKES 2 QUARTS * PREP/COOK TIME: 45 MINUTES, PLUS CHILLING AND FREEZING

Rocky road ice cream is an all-American classic if there ever was one, developed during the Depression to help lift the spirits of a down-trodden nation. Chocolate ice cream studded with toasted nuts and marsh-mallow bits makes this a modern favorite, as well. It's like a sundae in one chocolaty scoop! Swap out the pecans for any of your favorite nuts and it will still be a winner.

5 ounces bittersweet chocolate, chopped

8 extra-large egg yolks

1½ cups half-and-half

1 cup sugar

3 cups heavy (whipping) cream

1 teaspoon pure vanilla extract

Generous pinch kosher salt

2 cups chopped pecans

2 cups mini marshmallows

PREP

Put the chocolate in a medium heat-proof bowl and set aside.

Fill a large heat-proof bowl halfway with ice and place a fine-mesh strainer nearby.

In a small heat-proof bowl, whisk the egg yolks to combine. Set aside.

MAKE THE BASE

In a heavy-bottomed 4-quart pot over medium heat, combine the half-and-half and sugar. Heat the mixture, stirring occasionally with a heat-proof spatula to dissolve the sugar, until it is steamy and hot. Do not allow the mixture to boil.

When the liquid is hot, temper the egg yolks by pouring 1 cup of the hot liquid into the yolks in a slow, steady stream, whisking constantly. Immediately pour the tempered yolks into the pot, whisking constantly to combine. Scrape out the bowl that contained the egg yolks, using a heat-proof spatula.

Lower the heat under the pot slightly, and use the spatula to stir and scrape the bottom of the pot to keep the yolks from scrambling.

Continue to gently cook the custard base, stirring constantly and adjusting the heat if necessary, until the base begins to thicken and evenly coats the spatula. This should take about 5 minutes.

Strain the base through the fine-mesh strainer into the bowl with the chopped chocolate. Slowly whisk the custard and chocolate together until smooth. Stir in the heavy cream, vanilla, and salt until well mixed. Nestle the bowl into the readied ice bath and stir to cool down the mixture. Thoroughly chill the base over the ice, or cover the bowl with plastic wrap and refrigerate for at least 2 hours, or preferably overnight.

FREEZE

Place a 2-quart container with a tight-fitting lid in the freezer to chill. Freeze the ice cream according to your ice cream maker's instructions.

TOAST THE PECANS

While the base is freezing, toast the pecans. Preheat the oven to 350°F.

Line a baking sheet with parchment paper and lay out the chopped pecans on the sheet in a single layer. Toast the pecans, occasionally giving them a stir, until crispy, 12 to 14 minutes. Set aside to cool.

Fold the pecans and marshmallows into the finished ice cream as you are filling the chilled storage container.

 Choose the best-quality chocolate you can find and you will be rewarded with a delicious ice cream. For an edgier flavor, you can use 1 ounce unsweetened chocolate and 4 ounces bittersweet chocolate. If you do not have mini marshmallows, use a pair of lightly oiled scissors to cut large marshmallows into small pieces.

NEAPOLITAN
BOMBE

SERVES 12 * PREP TIME: 15 MINUTES, PLUS FREEZING

Naples, the capitol of the southern Italian region of Campania, is the origin of this molded ice cream dessert. The traditional colors of this confection were red, white, and green, representing an edible Italian flag. Flavors like cherry, vanilla, and pistachio were readily available to ice cream makers even in the mid-nineteenth century, making this dessert easy to accomplish. Fast-forward to our American version, where we have replaced the cherry with strawberry, vanilla endures, and chocolate has usurped pistachio.

Canola oil

1 quart Strawberry Ice Cream (page 36)

1 quart Dark Chocolate Ice Cream (page 67)

1 quart Madagascar Vanilla Ice Cream (page 34)

Ladyfingers or sponge cake (optional)

Kirschwasser, for soaking (optional)

Brush the interior of two $8\frac{1}{2}$-by-$4\frac{1}{2}$-inch loaf pans with canola oil. Line the pans with plastic wrap, leaving a 2-inch border of wrap overhanging all sides of the pans. Smooth out the wrinkles and push the wrap neatly into the corners.

Layer the bottom third of each loaf pan with strawberry ice cream. Smooth the layer with an offset spatula or the back of a spoon. Place the loaf pans in the freezer for at least 2 hours.

Layer the middle third of the loaf pans with chocolate ice cream. Smooth the layer with an offset spatula or the back of a spoon. Place the loaf pans in the freezer for another 2 hours.

Fill the rest of the loaf pans with vanilla ice cream. Smooth the top using an offset spatula or the back of a spoon. Give each loaf pan two or three raps on the countertop to compact the ice cream and force out any trapped air pockets.

Trim the ladyfingers (if using) to fit neatly in the loaf pans and gently press them into the vanilla ice cream layer. Soak the ladyfingers with Kirschwasser (if using).

Fold the excess plastic wrap over the top of the loaf pans to completely cover the bombes. Freeze them overnight.

To serve, unwrap the plastic from the top of the bombes and invert each bombe onto a wooden cutting board lined with parchment. The ladyfinger layer (if used) is now

on the bottom. Remove the loaf pan and discard the plastic wrap. Cut thick slices of the bombes to serve.

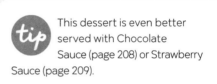
This dessert is even better served with Chocolate Sauce (page 208) or Strawberry Sauce (page 209).

ICE CREAM SANDWICHES

MAKES 16 ICE CREAM SANDWICHES * PREP TIME: 10 MINUTES. PLUS FREEZING

Our hearts race when we think of all the possible ice cream sandwich variations. Use your own favorite cookie recipe or our Chocolate Wafer Cookies (page 217) to deliver a one-two punch of frosty fun to your mouth. Slightly underbake the cookies, since biting into a crisp cookie filled with ice cream causes the filling to squeeze out of the back. Storing the assembled sandwiches overnight in the freezer will also help soften the cookie to a perfect eating texture. The idea is to have a bite of ice cream with every bite of cookie.

1 quart Peanut Butter Ice Cream (page 134) or Caramel Ice Cream (page 41)

32 Chocolate Wafer Cookies (page 217) or other cookies such as gingersnaps, chocolate chip, or peanut butter

Chopped Candied Nuts (page 203), crumbled All-American Peanut Brittle (page 204), or chopped toffee from Hokey Pokey Ice Cream (page 53), for garnish (optional)

PREP

Using a $\frac{1}{4}$-cup ice cream scoop, place a scoop of ice cream on the flat bottom of each of 16 cookies. Top each sandwich with a second cookie and then gently press the cookies together slightly to seal with the ice cream.

FREEZE

Place the sandwiches on a parchment paper–lined baking sheet and cover them with plastic wrap. Place the sheet in the freezer for 2 hours, or until firm.

Roll the exposed ice cream edges of each sandwich in your choice of garnish (if using) and return them to the freezer until ready to serve.

MAPLE WALNUT
ICE CREAM

MAKES 2 QUARTS * PREP/COOK TIME: 45 MINUTES,
PLUS CHILLING AND FREEZING

Maple syrup is one of nature's most delicious gifts; there isn't anything like it. Yes, it is expensive, but that's because it takes about 40 gallons of maple sap to produce 1 gallon of this divine golden liquid. There is no substitution worthy of real maple syrup. We suggest using Grade B maple syrup, which has a deeper flavor and darker color.

4½ cups heavy (whipping) cream

12 extra-large egg yolks

2¼ cups half-and-half

3 tablespoons sugar

1 to 1½ cups pure maple syrup

¼ teaspoon pure vanilla extract

Generous pinch kosher salt

1½ cups walnuts

MAKE THE BASE

Fill a large heat-proof bowl halfway with ice. Nestle a smaller heat-proof bowl in the ice and place a fine-mesh strainer over it. Add the heavy cream to the smaller of the chilled bowls. Set aside.

In a small heat-proof bowl, whisk the egg yolks to combine. Set aside.

In a heavy-bottomed 4-quart pot over medium heat, combine the half-and-half and sugar. Heat the mixture, stirring occasionally with a heat-proof spatula to dissolve the sugar, until it is steamy and hot. Do not allow the mixture to boil.

When the liquid is hot, temper the egg yolks by pouring 1 cup of the hot liquid into the yolks in a slow, steady stream, whisking constantly. Immediately pour the tempered yolks into the pot, whisking constantly to combine. Scrape out the bowl that contained the egg yolks, using a heat-proof spatula.

Lower the heat under the pot slightly, and use the spatula to stir and scrape the bottom of the pot to keep the yolks from scrambling. Continue to gently cook the custard base, stirring constantly and adjusting the heat if necessary, until the base begins to thicken and evenly coats the spatula. This should take about 5 minutes.

Strain the base into the chilled heavy cream. Stir the mixture to stop the cooking process and to combine the custard and cream. Stir in the maple syrup, vanilla, and salt. Thoroughly chill the base over the ice, or cover the bowl with plastic wrap and refrigerate for at least 2 hours, or preferably overnight.

FREEZE

Place a 2-quart container with a tight-fitting lid in the freezer to chill. Freeze the ice cream according to your ice cream maker's instructions.

TOAST THE WALNUTS

While the base is freezing, toast the walnuts. Preheat the oven to 350°F.

Line a baking sheet with parchment paper and lay out the walnuts on the sheet in a single layer. Toast the walnuts, occasionally giving them a stir, until crispy, 12 to 14 minutes. Once they are cool enough to handle, rub them between your fingers and palms to loosen any skin that wants to come off. Walnut skins can be bitter, so this is an important step. Roughly chop the walnuts and set aside.

Fold the walnuts into the finished ice cream as you are filling the chilled storage container.

tip Pecans are a delicious substitute for walnuts.

CHERRY
ICE POPS

MAKES 6 TO 8 ICE POPS * PREP/COOK TIME: 30 MINUTES, PLUS CHILLING AND FREEZING

Cherry is the most popular flavor for ice pops and has been for generations. Here is our version, born out of the avalanche of cherries that descends upon the farmers' markets each spring.

6 tablespoons water

6 tablespoons sugar, plus more if needed

Generous pinch kosher salt

1 pound Bing cherries, pitted

Few drops freshly squeezed lemon juice

PREP

Freeze your ice pop molds according to the manufacturer's instructions.

MAKE THE BASE

In a small saucepot over high heat, combine the water, sugar, and salt and bring to a boil, stirring occasionally to dissolve the sugar completely. Remove the syrup from the heat and set aside to cool slightly.

Put the pitted cherries and lemon juice in a food processor or blender. Pour in $\frac{1}{2}$ cup of the warm syrup and purée until smooth. Strain the purée through a medium-mesh strainer into a small bowl, pressing on the fruit to extract as much liquid as possible. Taste the purée and adjust the sweetness with up to $\frac{1}{4}$ cup of the remaining syrup (if not sweet enough) or a few additional drops of lemon juice (if it is too sweet). The mixture should be very sweet, as the sweetness will be somewhat diluted when frozen. Cover the bowl with plastic wrap and chill thoroughly in the refrigerator.

FREEZE

Fill the chilled ice pop molds with the ice pop mixture, and freeze.

MILKSHAKE

MAKES 1 (12-OUNCE) MILKSHAKE * PREP TIME: 5 MINUTES

Almost any ice cream can be turned into a rich, delicious milkshake. Somehow adding ice-cold milk and a few drops of vanilla extract to scoops of ice cream, then blending it, miraculously amplifies the intrinsic flavors. Maybe it is how you enjoy a shake that makes it taste so good? A straw delivers the thick, frosty drink right to your taste buds. Or is a spoon the way to go?

1 cup Toasted Almond Ice Cream (page 43), Dark Chocolate Ice Cream (page 67), or Strawberry Ice Cream (page 36)

½ cup whole milk, very cold

Few drops pure vanilla extract

Perfectly Whipped Cream (page 207, optional)

Scoop the ice cream into a tall-sided plastic container or glass measuring cup. Add the cold milk and vanilla. Using an immersion blender, purée the ice cream until it is thick, yet pourable. Pour the milkshake into a tall glass and top with whipped cream (if using). If you prefer a thicker shake, use a little more ice cream.

 We use an immersion blender to quickly bring together our shakes. A countertop blender works as well, although it may produce a frothier finished product.

VANILLA-ORANGE
ICE POPS

MAKES 6 TO 8 ICE POPS * PREP TIME: 5 MINUTES, PLUS FREEZING

Freshly squeezed orange juice meets exotic vanilla in this throwback ice pop. Use organic juice oranges such as Valencia, or blend the juice with a bit of tangerine juice for a tangier pop. A high quality vanilla extract, one that uses Madagascar vanilla, preferably organic, is worth the extra pennies.

1½ cups freshly squeezed orange juice, such as Valencia

3 tablespoons half-and-half

½ teaspoon pure vanilla extract, or more to taste

¼ cup sugar, or more to taste

Generous pinch kosher salt

PREP

Freeze your ice pop molds according to the manufacturer's instructions.

MAKE THE BASE

In a small bowl, stir together the orange juice, half-and-half, vanilla, sugar, and salt until the sugar is dissolved. Taste the mixture and adjust it if needed with more sugar or vanilla. It should be very sweet, as freezing will dull the brightness slightly.

FREEZE

Fill the chilled ice pop molds with the ice pop mixture, and freeze.

BANANA SPLIT

The banana split, the icon of the 1950s American soda fountain if there ever was one, will be the crown jewel of any ice cream social. Once you have gathered the necessary ingredients, building the layers is easy. Do not be put off by the size of a typical banana split; simply choose a smaller dish and downsize the portions. The fun remains even with fewer calories. If you want to make a big impression, find attractive metal or glass serving boats and matching silver spoons. This one's all about presentation, no matter the size.

Peel and halve the bananas lengthwise. Place two banana slices in each of two banana split boats.

Place 1 scoop each of strawberry, vanilla, and chocolate ice creams between the banana slices.

Drizzle the strawberry ice cream with strawberry sauce, the vanilla ice cream with caramelized pineapple, and the chocolate ice cream with chocolate sauce.

Top each banana split with a generous dollop of whipped cream, sprinkle the nuts over the whipped cream, and garnish each split with roasted cherries (if using).

2 ripe bananas

1 quart Strawberry Ice Cream (page 36)

1 quart Madagascar Vanilla Ice Cream (page 34)

1 quart Dark Chocolate Ice Cream (page 67)

Strawberry Sauce (page 209)

Warm Caramelized Pineapple
    with Rum (page 210)

Chocolate Sauce (page 208)

Perfectly Whipped Cream (page 207)

Chopped Candied Nuts (page 203)

Roasted Cherries (page 216, optional)

BROWN COW
(ROOT BEER FLOAT)

MAKES 1 (12-OUNCE) FLOAT * PREP TIME: 5 MINUTES

Serious controversy surrounds the moniker brown cow: Some swear it is vanilla ice cream and root beer. Others expect chocolate ice cream and root beer, while still others add chocolate syrup and call *that* a brown cow. Wherever you stand, we've got you covered. Opt for an artisanal root beer, one that contains cane sugar rather than high-fructose corn syrup, and that lacks artificial flavors and colors.

Drizzle a bit of chocolate sauce (if using) in a tall pint or float glass. Fill the glass with root beer. Gently place a generous scoop of ice cream into the root beer and top with whipped cream (if using). Serve with a straw, long-handled spoon, and plenty of napkins.

Chocolate Sauce (page 208, optional)

12 ounces root beer, very cold

Madagascar Vanilla Ice Cream (page 34) or
    Dark Chocolate Ice Cream (page 67)

Perfectly Whipped Cream (page 207, optional)

ICE CREAM SUNDAE

MAKES 1 SUNDAE ✻ PREP TIME: 5 MINUTES

Sundaes—artful, edible creations—should be visually appealing, so flex your inner soda jerk and have fun, then dazzle guests with your creation. This is less of a recipe and more of a guideline for making a sundae. We will refrain from preaching about flavor combinations and toppings that should or should not be present, but there *is* a winning combination here. Really, it just comes down to one or two ice cream flavors, a sauce, and a topping. Or two. Or three.

Chocolate Sauce (page 208), Strawberry Sauce (page 209), Creamy Caramel Sauce (page 201), Butterscotch Sauce (page 200), or Hot Fudge Sauce (page 202)

Candied Nuts (page 203, optional)

2 scoops favorite ice cream

Perfectly Whipped Cream (page 207)

Roasted Cherries (page 216, optional)

Chill a wide-mouthed ice cream dish, coupe, or sundae cup. This will keep the ice cream from melting too quickly.

Drizzle some sauce in the bottom of the glass. Add some candied nuts (if using). Place 2 well-rounded scoops of ice cream in the dish. Drizzle more sauce over the ice cream and top it with a generous dollop of whipped cream. Sprinkle more candied nuts (if using) over everything and garnish with a roasted cherry (if using). Serve with a long-handled spoon.

PEACHES AND CREAM

MAKES 2 QUARTS * PREP TIME: 20 MINUTES, PLUS FREEZING

When the summer peaches arrive, it is time for this special treat. We take this one step further and serve it with raspberry sauce for a version of one of our all-time favorite desserts, peach Melba. This combination comes together so wonderfully and naturally, you will want to make this several times during peach season. Layering the sherbet and ice cream in the container makes for a nice-looking swirled scoop.

1 quart Madagascar Vanilla Ice Cream (page 34)

1 quart Peach Sherbet (page 96)

2 pints ripe raspberries, divided

Sugar, for sweetening

Sliced fresh peaches, for garnish

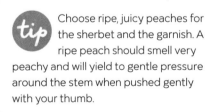 **tip** Choose ripe, juicy peaches for the sherbet and the garnish. A ripe peach should smell very peachy and will yield to gentle pressure around the stem when pushed gently with your thumb.

Place a 2-quart container with a tight-fitting lid in the freezer.

Once the container is chilled, alternate layers of vanilla ice cream and peach sherbet in the container, smoothing each layer evenly with an offset spatula or the back of a spoon. Make the layers only about ½ inch thick so that you get several layers of both flavors in every scoop. Freeze for several hours or overnight.

To prepare the raspberry sauce, purée 1½ pints of raspberries in a blender or food processor. Strain the purée through a fine-mesh strainer into a small bowl. Taste the purée and sweeten it with a bit of sugar, if needed. Cover the bowl with plastic wrap and refrigerate until ready to serve.

To serve, pour a little raspberry purée into chilled coupes or dishes, place two scoops of layered ice cream on top, and garnish with a few slices of fresh peach and a few fresh raspberries.

CONCORD GRAPE
SHERBET

MAKES 1 QUART * PREP/COOK TIME: 30 MINUTES, PLUS CHILLING AND FREEZING

It is hard to say goodbye to the summer fruits as fall inches its way in, but when the Concord grapes show up, it eases the pain. Concords are beautiful grapes, purple and blue, all frosty and plump. Their aroma is distinctive and so is their flavor. They are very plum-like in that the skin is strong and tart, but the flesh is soft and sweet. This sherbet is just pure Concord flavor, and spins into a lovely color. It pairs well with Pear Sherbet (page 95) and, yes, even with Peanut Butter Ice Cream (page 134).

3 pounds Concord grapes

⅓ cup water

3 tablespoons sugar

2 tablespoons corn syrup

PREP

Wash the grapes and pick them off their stems. (If you have a standing electric mixer with a dough hook, you can put the grape bunches in the work bowl and set the speed to low. The action of the hook does a pretty good job at stemming the grapes.)

MAKE THE BASE

Place the grapes in a stainless-steel pot over medium heat, add the water, cover the pot, and simmer, stirring occasionally until the fruit is tender, about 10 minutes.

Using a food mill with the smallest plate, mill the grapes, then pass them and any liquid from the pot through a fine-mesh strainer into a bowl to collect any seed bits that remain.

Transfer 1 quart of grape juice to a medium bowl. Add the sugar and corn syrup and mix until the sugar is dissolved. Cover the bowl with plastic wrap and refrigerate to chill thoroughly for at least 2 hours, or preferably overnight.

FREEZE

Place a 1-quart container with a tight-fitting lid in your freezer to chill. Freeze the chilled sherbet base according to your ice cream maker's instructions. Store the finished sherbet in the chilled container.

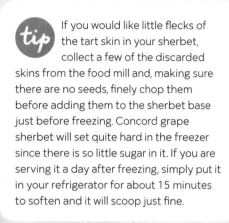

If you would like little flecks of the tart skin in your sherbet, collect a few of the discarded skins from the food mill and, making sure there are no seeds, finely chop them before adding them to the sherbet base just before freezing. Concord grape sherbet will set quite hard in the freezer since there is so little sugar in it. If you are serving it a day after freezing, simply put it in your refrigerator for about 15 minutes to soften and it will scoop just fine.

surprising

The flavors and ingredients featured in this chapter may be a bit left of center, but from time to time the tried and true just will not do. On those occasions when you want to add a wrinkle to a sundae or pair a contrasting taste alongside a familiar classic, look no further than these unexpected flavors. Since almost every culture enjoys frozen desserts, we have adapted an assortment of recipes representing the four corners of the globe. We stamped our passports so you don't have to!

RICE
ICE CREAM

MAKES 1¼ QUARTS * PREP/COOK TIME: 1 HOUR, PLUS CHILLING AND FREEZING

Italian cooks are notorious for incorporating ingredients they cherish across all courses of a meal, interchanging sweet and savory elements with great success. A stellar example of this "blurring" is risotto ice cream. Starchy, slightly chewy, plump rice grains are suspended in a rich, egg custard. Think about how delightfully satisfying a bowl of rice pudding can be; the same idea is in play here. This ice cream is most delicious eaten the day it is frozen.

3½ cups whole milk, divided

9 tablespoons sugar, divided

1 Madagascar vanilla bean, split lengthwise

¾ teaspoon kosher salt

½ cup arborio rice

2 cups heavy (whipping) cream

3 extra-large egg yolks

1 tablespoon confectioners' sugar

PREP

In a heavy-bottomed 2-quart saucepan over medium heat, combine 3 cups of milk, 3 tablespoons of sugar, the vanilla bean, and the salt. Bring the liquid to a simmer and stir in the rice. Lower the heat to maintain a steady, gentle simmer and cook the rice, stirring often to keep it from sticking to the bottom of the pan, until completely tender, 12 to 15 minutes. Place a fine-mesh strainer over a medium bowl and pour the rice and liquid into the strainer. Allow the mixture to cool and drain for 30 minutes.

MAKE THE BASE

While the rice is draining, prepare the custard. Fill a large heat-proof bowl halfway with ice. Nestle a smaller heat-proof bowl in the ice and place a fine-mesh strainer over it. Add the heavy cream to the smaller of the chilled bowls. Set aside

In a small heat-proof bowl, whisk the egg yolks to combine. Set aside.

In a small saucepan over medium heat, combine the remaining ½ cup of milk and 6 tablespoons of sugar. Heat the milk, stirring occasionally with a heat-proof spatula to dissolve the sugar, until it is steamy and hot. Do not allow the mixture to boil.

When the liquid is hot, temper the egg yolks by pouring about $\frac{1}{4}$ cup of the hot liquid into the yolks in a slow, steady stream, whisking constantly. Immediately pour the tempered yolks into the pot, whisking constantly to combine. Scrape out the bowl that contained the egg yolks, using a heat-proof spatula.

Lower the heat under the pot slightly, and use the spatula to stir and scrape the bottom of the pot to keep the yolks from scrambling. Continue to gently cook the custard base, stirring constantly and adjusting the heat if necessary, until the base begins to thicken and evenly coats the spatula. This should take about 5 minutes.

Strain the base into the chilled heavy cream. Do not scrape out the pot. Stir the mixture to stop the cooking process and to combine the custard and cream. Whisk in the powdered sugar. Stir in the drained rice (discard the vanilla bean). Cover the bowl with plastic wrap and thoroughly chill the custard base in the refrigerator for at least 2 hours, or preferably overnight.

FREEZE

Place a 2-quart container with a tight-fitting lid in the freezer to chill. Freeze the ice cream base according to your ice cream maker's instructions. It's best to eat this ice cream the same day it is made. Keep it in the chilled container until ready to serve.

 Arborio rice is a short- to medium-grain plump, somewhat oval-shaped rice that has high starch content. It hails from the Po River valley of Northern Italy. If you cannot find arborio rice, use carnaroli, which is widely available. Never rinse risotto rice prior to cooking; the starch lends a desirable creaminess to all dishes.

FIOR DI LATTE
ICE CREAM (MILK FLOWER)

MAKES 3 QUARTS * PREP/COOK TIME: 10 MINUTES, PLUS CHILLING AND FREEZING

Italy's artisan gelateria offerings challenge the senses in the best possible ways. Choices range from the familiar to the silly, some slightly bewildering while others whimsically fictitious. What could be more enticing than ice cream delicately harvested from the flowers of milk (*fior di latte*)?

5¼ cups plus 2 tablespoons whole milk

3 cups plus 2 tablespoons heavy (whipping) cream

¾ cup plus 2 tablespoons corn syrup

1 cup plus 2 tablespoons sugar

¾ cup plus 2 tablespoons powdered milk

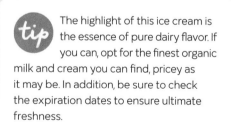

tip The highlight of this ice cream is the essence of pure dairy flavor. If you can, opt for the finest organic milk and cream you can find, pricey as it may be. In addition, be sure to check the expiration dates to ensure ultimate freshness.

MAKE THE BASE

Fill a large heat-proof bowl halfway with ice. Nestle a smaller heat-proof bowl in the ice and place a fine-mesh strainer over it.

In a large pot over medium-low heat, combine the milk, cream, corn syrup, and sugar. Heat the mixture, stirring often with a heat-proof spatula to dissolve the sugar and corn syrup. Do not let the liquid boil. When the sugars are dissolved, whisk in the powdered milk until no lumps remain.

Strain the ice cream base into the chilled bowl setup. Do not scrape out the pot. Stir it to stop the cooking process. Cover the bowl with plastic wrap and chill thoroughly in the refrigerator for at least 2 hours, or preferably overnight.

FREEZE

Place one large or two small containers with tight-fitting lids in the freezer to chill. Freeze the ice cream base according to your ice cream maker's instructions. Store the finished ice cream in the chilled container(s).

CREMA
ICE CREAM

MAKES 2 QUARTS * PREP/COOK TIME: 30 MINUTES, PLUS CHILLING AND FREEZING

The focus of this richly simple ice cream is the exceptional dairy ingredients that unite to produce a surprisingly complex frozen treat. The literal translation would be "cream ice cream," which in and of itself sounds tempting. As with other minimalist recipes, the highest-quality ingredients you can procure are in order.

5 extra-large eggs

1 extra-large egg yolk

1½ cups sugar

2 cups whole milk

1½ cups heavy (whipping) cream, ideally not ultra-pasteurized

⅓ cup corn syrup

1 Madagascar vanilla bean

MAKE THE BASE

Fill a large heat-proof bowl halfway with ice. Nestle a smaller heat-proof bowl in the ice and place a fine-mesh strainer over it.

Combine the eggs, egg yolk, and sugar in the bowl of a standing electric mixer fixed with the whisk attachment. Beat on medium speed until light, pale and voluminous, 8 to 10 minutes. Turn the mixer speed to the lowest setting and continue beating the eggs while you prepare the ice cream base.

In a heavy-bottomed 4-quart pot over medium-high heat, combine the milk, heavy cream, and corn syrup. With a paring knife, split the vanilla bean lengthwise, scrape out the seeds, and add the seeds and pod to the warming liquid. Heat the liquid, stirring occasionally with a heat-proof spatula to dissolve the sugar and corn syrup and to distribute the vanilla seeds evenly. Bring the liquid just to a simmer and immediately turn the heat to low to keep the liquid from boiling over. >>

Stop the mixer. Using a heat-proof spatula, quickly stir the whipped eggs and sugar mixture into the simmering liquid. Scrape out the bowl thoroughly while evenly incorporating the eggs into the cream. Continuously stir and scrape the bottom of the pot to avoid scrambling the eggs, 2 to 3 minutes.

Strain the custard into the chilled bowl and discard the vanilla pod. Do not scrape out the pot or press any solids through the strainer. Stir the custard in the chilled bowl to stop the cooking process. Once cooled, cover the bowl with plastic wrap and chill thoroughly in the refrigerator for at least 2 hours, or preferably overnight.

FREEZE

Place a 2-quart container with a tight-fitting lid in the freezer to chill. Freeze the ice cream base according to your ice cream maker's instructions. Store the finished ice cream in the chilled container.

EGGLESS
ICE CREAM BASE

MAKES 2 QUARTS * PREP/COOK TIME: 10 MINUTES, PLUS CHILLING AND FREEZING

This is a wonderful "neutral" ice cream base that can be used as a starting point for incorporating a variety of flavors. Keep a batch of this eggless base in your refrigerator, and let inspiration move you in the form of a generous pour of alcohol, fruit purée, or Italian syrup. There is hardly a wrong way to go. This base is similar to the base for Fior di Latte Ice Cream (page 130), but the additional dairy in that recipe sets it apart. Powdered milk is a key component to this recipe and is available from online retailers and at Whole Foods Market.

4¼ cups whole milk

2 cups heavy (whipping) cream

¾ cup corn syrup

1 cup plus 2 tablespoons sugar

¾ cup plus 2 tablespoons powdered milk

In a large pot over medium-low heat, combine the milk, cream, corn syrup, and sugar. Heat the liquid, stirring often with a heat-proof spatula to dissolve the sugar and corn syrup, until it is hot and steamy, about 5 minutes. Do not let the liquid boil. When the sugars are dissolved, whisk in the powdered milk until no lumps remain.

Strain the base into a 3-quart container with a tight-fitting lid. Chill completely in the refrigerator for at least 2 hours, or preferably overnight.

The base is now ready to be flavored with syrups, fruit purées, or alcohol combinations of your choosing. The base can be refrigerated for up to a week before being frozen.

 This recipe is a great example of making a recipe "to taste" or "taste and adjust." Tasting the base before, during, and after making it will familiarize your palate with how flavors build and change prior to freezing. Keep in mind that flavors are slightly muted when frozen, so be bold with the flavor combinations you use.

PEANUT BUTTER
ICE CREAM

MAKES 2 QUARTS ∗ PREP/COOK TIME: 20 MINUTES, PLUS CHILLING AND FREEZING

This flavor seems classic American to us, so why is it in the "Surprising" chapter? Because it's surprising how delicious and balanced peanut butter ice cream can be—creamy and salty with a slightly fatty mouthfeel. A giant scoop of peanut butter ice cream atop a sugar cone and a lazy Sunday spent exploring the flea market, and we are 10 years old all over again.

4 cups heavy (whipping) cream

12 extra-large egg yolks

2 cups half-and-half

1⅓ cups sugar

¾ cup plus 1 tablespoon creamy peanut butter

MAKE THE BASE

Fill a large heat-proof bowl halfway with ice. Nestle a smaller heat-proof bowl in the ice and place a fine-mesh strainer over it. Add the heavy cream to the smaller of the chilled bowls. Set aside.

In a small heat-proof bowl, whisk the egg yolks to combine. Set aside.

In a heavy-bottomed 4-quart pot over medium-low heat, combine the half-and-half and sugar. Heat the mixture, stirring occasionally with a heat-proof spatula to dissolve the sugar, until it is steamy and hot. Do not allow the mixture to boil.

When the liquid is hot, temper the egg yolks by pouring 1 cup of the liquid into the yolks in a slow, steady stream, whisking constantly. Immediately pour the tempered yolks into the pot, whisking constantly to combine. Scrape out the bowl that contained the egg yolks, using a heat-proof spatula.

Lower the heat under the pot slightly, and use the spatula to stir and scrape the bottom of the pot to keep the yolks from scrambling. Continue to gently cook the custard base, stirring constantly and adjusting the heat if necessary, until the base begins to thicken and evenly coats the spatula. This should take about 5 minutes.

Strain the base into the chilled heavy cream. Do not scrape out the pot. Stir the mixture to stop the cooking process and to combine the custard and cream.

Put the peanut butter in a large bowl. Whisk the custard base into the peanut butter, $\frac{1}{2}$ cup at a time, until it is smooth and no lumps remain. Cover the bowl with plastic wrap and thoroughly chill the base in the refrigerator for at least 2 hours, or preferably overnight.

FREEZE

Place a 2-quart container with a tight-fitting lid in the freezer to chill. Freeze the ice cream base according to your ice cream maker's instructions. Store the finished ice cream in the chilled container.

 Chocolate is a natural pairing for this ice cream, of course. After all, who doesn't love a peanut butter cup? For an extra bite of peanutty crunch, fold in crumbled All-American Peanut Brittle (page 204).

LONDON FOG
ICE CREAM

MAKES 1 QUART * PREP/COOK TIME: 45 MINUTES, PLUS CHILLING AND FREEZING

This is truly a surprising flavor. Earl Grey is a black tea flavored with the oil from bergamot, a citrus thought to be a hybrid of the Seville orange and sweet lemon or lime. It is a lovely, aromatic, lingering, and slightly haunting brew. This is our frozen version of the London Fog, which is Earl Grey tea with steamed milk and vanilla syrup. This ice cream goes well with simple butter cake, dried fruit compote, or a delicate chocolate cake.

3 cups heavy (whipping) cream

8 extra-large egg yolks

1¾ cups half-and-half

1 cup plus 2 tablespoons sugar

6 tablespoons Earl Grey tea leaves

Few drops pure vanilla extract

MAKE THE BASE

Fill a large heat-proof bowl halfway with ice. Nestle a smaller heat-proof bowl in the ice and place a fine-mesh strainer over it. Add the heavy cream to the smaller of the chilled bowls. Set aside.

In a small heat-proof bowl, whisk the egg yolks to combine. Set aside.

In a heavy-bottomed 2-quart saucepan over medium-low heat, combine the half-and-half and sugar. Heat the mixture, stirring occasionally with a heat-proof spatula to dissolve the sugar, until it is steamy and hot. Do not allow the liquid to boil. Once the liquid is hot and the sugar dissolved, turn off the heat and stir in the tea leaves. Cover the pot and let the tea steep for 15 minutes.

Return the pot to the stove and rewarm the mixture over medium-low heat. When it is hot, temper the egg yolks by pouring about ½ cup of the hot liquid into the egg yolks in a slow, steady stream, whisking constantly. Immediately pour the tempered yolks into the pot, whisking constantly to combine. Scrape out the bowl that contained the egg yolks, using a heat-proof spatula.

Lower the heat under the pot slightly, and use the spatula to stir and scrape the bottom of the pot to keep the yolks from scrambling. Continue to gently cook the custard base, stirring constantly and adjusting the heat if necessary, until the base begins to thicken and evenly coats the spatula. This should take about 5 minutes.

Strain the base into the chilled heavy cream. Do not scrape out the pot. Add the vanilla and stir the mixture to stop the cooking process and to combine the custard and cream. Thoroughly chill the base over the ice, or cover the bowl with plastic wrap and refrigerate for at least 2 hours, or preferably overnight.

FREEZE

Place a 2-quart container with a tight-fitting lid in the freezer to chill. Freeze the ice cream base according to your ice cream maker's instructions. Store the finished ice cream in the chilled container.

 Avoid using tea bags, as the tea is usually crumbled and may be of poor quality, and there is no telling its freshness. Buy fresh, loose-leaf tea and you will be rewarded with a much more complex and true Earl Grey flavor.

RAS EL HANOUT
ICE CREAM

MAKES 2 QUARTS * PREP/COOK TIME: 1 HOUR, PLUS CHILLING AND FREEZING

Ras el hanout is a spice mix from North Africa, and its name means "head of the shop" or, in more familiar terms, "top shelf." The name suggests that the blend is made of the finest spices that particular shop has to offer, so no two shops will have exactly the same blend. Neat! This recipe is our top-shelf blend. Ras el hanout is largely used in savory cooking, so we've stayed on the sweet side of spices for this one.

2½ cups half-and-half

1⅓ cups sugar

1 (3-inch) cinnamon stick

12 black peppercorns

10 whole cloves, pounded slightly in a mortar or pulsed in a spice grinder

1 teaspoon fenugreek seed, pounded slightly in a mortar or pulsed in a spice grinder

½ teaspoon anise seed, pounded slightly in a mortar or pulsed in a spice grinder

1 teaspoon ground nutmeg

½ teaspoon ground ginger

½ teaspoon ground cardamom

½ teaspoon ground mace

4 cups heavy (whipping) cream

10 extra-large egg yolks

PREP

In a heavy-bottomed 4-quart pot over medium heat, combine the half-and-half and sugar. Heat the mixture, stirring occasionally with a heat-proof spatula to dissolve the sugar, until it is steamy and hot. Do not allow the mixture to boil. Add the cinnamon stick, peppercorns, cloves, fenugreek, anise, nutmeg, ginger, cardamom, and mace and mix thoroughly. Remove the pot from the heat, cover, and set aside for 30 minutes to steep.

MAKE THE BASE

Fill a large heat-proof bowl halfway with ice. Nestle a smaller heat-proof bowl in the ice and place a fine-mesh strainer over it. Add the heavy cream to the smaller of the chilled bowls. Set aside.

In a small heat-proof bowl, whisk the egg yolks to combine. Set aside.

Return the pot to the stove and rewarm the half-and-half over medium-low heat. When it is hot, temper the egg yolks by pouring 1 cup of the liquid into the egg yolks in a slow, steady stream, whisking constantly. Immediately pour the tempered yolks into the pot, whisking constantly to combine. Scrape out the bowl that contained the egg yolks, using a heat-proof spatula.

Lower the heat under the pot slightly, and use the spatula to stir and scrape the bottom of the pot to keep the yolks from scrambling. Continue to gently cook the custard base, stirring constantly and adjusting the heat if necessary, until the base begins to thicken and evenly coats the spatula. This should take about 5 minutes.

Strain the base into the chilled heavy cream. Do not scrape out the pot. Stir the mixture to stop the cooking process and to combine the custard and cream. Thoroughly chill the base over the ice, or cover the bowl with plastic wrap and refrigerate for at least 2 hours, or preferably overnight.

FREEZE

Place a 2-quart container with a tight-fitting lid in the freezer to chill. Freeze the ice cream base according to your ice cream maker's instructions. Store the finished ice cream in the chilled container.

tip

Remember, no two ras el hanout blends are alike, and this ice cream can easily be adjusted to suit your tastes. Stir in an extra pinch of cardamom, cinnamon, or nutmeg just before freezing the ice cream base if you want a particular flavor to be more forward. This ice cream pairs well with summer stone fruits like nectarines or plums.

SICILIAN BREAKFAST

MAKES 4 INDIVIDUAL GLASSES ✳ PREP TIME: 20 MINUTES

This is a play on the traditional morning ritual for millions of Italians: cappuccino and a flaky pastry. Brewed espresso, in this case in the form of a granita, meets frothy steamed milk, which is represented by rich Crema Ice Cream (page 131), then crowned by a warm buttery brioche. It demonstrates how crazy Italians are for gelato and granita. This confection is typically enjoyed mid-morning, somewhere between having a cappuccino and easing into an espresso.

1 recipe Espresso Granita (page 52)

1 quart Crema Ice Cream (page 131)

4 individual brioches or croissants

Preheat the oven to 325°F.

Chill four 8-ounce glasses in the freezer.

Place the granita and ice cream in the refrigerator to slightly soften, 10 to 15 minutes.

Place the pastries on a baking sheet and warm in the oven.

When the pastry is warm and the frozen items have softened sufficiently, remove the glasses from the freezer. Fill the bottom half of each glass with granita. Fill the top half of the glass with ice cream. Serve the warm pastry alongside the glass or, more properly, placed on top of the ice cream.

To eat, tear off pieces of warm pastry and scoop up the cold ice cream. Finish by enjoying the slushy espresso granita.

ORANGE-CARDAMOM
ICE CREAM

MAKES 2 QUARTS * PREP/COOK TIME: 45 MINUTES TO 1 HOUR,
PLUS CHILLING AND FREEZING

Cardamom is a staple in Indian cooking and has a unique, earthy aroma. It is used extensively in savory and sweet dishes as well as to flavor coffee and tea. Guatemala and India are the largest producers. This ice cream pairs exceptionally well with a simple pistachio butter cake and fresh sliced oranges.

1½ cups half-and-half

1 cup sugar

Zest of 1 large orange

10 cardamom pods, lightly crushed

3 cups heavy (whipping) cream

8 extra-large egg yolks

Generous pinch kosher salt

PREP

In a heavy-bottomed 4-quart pot over medium heat, combine the half-and-half and sugar. Heat the mixture, stirring occasionally with a heat-proof spatula to dissolve the sugar, until it is steamy and hot. Do not allow the mixture to boil. Stir in the zest and cardamom. Turn off the heat, cover the pot, and set aside for 20 minutes to steep. Taste the mixture. If you would like a stronger flavor, let it steep for 10 minutes more.

MAKE THE BASE

Fill a large heat-proof bowl halfway with ice. Nestle a smaller heat-proof bowl in the ice and place a fine-mesh strainer over it. Add the heavy cream to the smaller of the chilled bowls. Set aside.

In a small heat-proof bowl, whisk the egg yolks to combine. Set aside.

Return the pot to the stove and rewarm the half-and-half over medium-low heat. When it is hot, temper the egg yolks by pouring 1 cup of the hot liquid into the egg yolks in a slow, steady stream, whisking constantly. Immediately pour the tempered yolks into the pot, whisking constantly to combine. Scrape out the bowl that contained the egg yolks, using a heat-proof spatula.

Lower the heat under the pot slightly, and use the spatula to stir and scrape the bottom of the pot to keep the yolks from scrambling. Continue to gently cook the custard base, stirring constantly and adjusting the heat if necessary, until the base begins to thicken and evenly coats the spatula. This should take about 5 minutes.

Strain the base into the chilled heavy cream. Do not scrape out the pot. Stir to stop the cooking process and to combine the custard and cream. Stir in the salt. Thoroughly chill the ice cream base over the ice, or cover the bowl with plastic wrap and refrigerate for at least 2 hours, or preferably overnight.

FREEZE

Place a 2-quart container with a tight-fitting lid in the freezer to chill. Freeze the chilled ice cream base according to your ice cream maker's instructions. Store the finished ice cream in the chilled container.

tip To add a little more flavor and a beautiful fleck to your finished ice cream, stir in some additional finely grated fresh orange zest and a pinch of ground cardamom or cinnamon to the base just before spinning.

HONEY-LAVENDER
ICE CREAM

MAKES 2 QUARTS * PREP/COOK TIME: 45 MINUTES TO 1 HOUR, PLUS CHILLING AND FREEZING

Honey and lavender are two eso- teric, perfumed, natural flavors. When paired with sweetened cream, the result is a creamy con- fection that highlights the nuances of each special ingredient. There are dozens, if not hundreds of hon- eys available, but we especially like thistle honey for use here. It is light and floral; when combined with strong-scented lavender, it adds richness without creating a flower bomb.

4½ cups heavy (whipping) cream

12 extra-large egg yolks

2¼ cups half-and-half

¾ cup sugar

Generous pinch kosher salt

2 tablespoons fresh lavender flowers

½ cup plus 3 tablespoons honey, preferably thistle, warmed slightly

MAKE THE BASE

Fill a large heat-proof bowl halfway with ice. Nestle a smaller heat-proof bowl in the ice and place a fine-mesh strainer over it. Add the heavy cream to the smaller of the chilled bowls. Set aside.

In a small heat-proof bowl, whisk the egg yolks to combine. Set aside.

In a heavy-bottomed 4-quart pot over medium-low heat, combine the half-and-half, sugar, and salt, stirring occasionally with a heat-proof spatula, to dissolve the sugar, until steamy and hot. Do not allow the mixture to boil. When the half-and-half is hot, stir in the lavender. Remove the pot from the heat, cover it, and set aside for 15 minutes to steep. Taste and con- tinue to steep in 10-minute intervals until the lavender flavor is perceptible but not overwhelming.

Return the pot to the stove and rewarm the half-and-half over medium-low heat. When it is hot, temper the egg yolks by pouring 1 cup of the hot liquid into the egg yolks in a slow, steady stream, whisking constantly. Immediately pour the tempered yolks into the pot, whisking constantly to combine. Scrape out the bowl that contained the egg yolks, using a heat-proof spatula.

Lower the heat under the pot slightly, and use the spatula to stir and scrape the bottom of the pot to keep the yolks from scrambling. Continue to gently cook the custard base, stirring constantly and adjusting the heat if necessary, until the base begins to thicken and evenly coats the spatula. This should take about 5 minutes.

Strain the base into the chilled heavy cream. Do not scrape out the pot. Stir the mixture to stop the cooking process and to combine the custard and cream. If you desire, add the strained-out lavender flowers to the liquid for a more intense flower flavor. Stir the warmed honey into the custard base and mix well. Thoroughly chill the ice cream base over the ice, or cover the bowl with plastic wrap and refrigerate for at least 2 hours, or preferably overnight.

FREEZE

Place a 2-quart container with a tight-fitting lid in the freezer to chill. Remove any remaining lavender flowers from the ice cream base and freeze the base according to your ice cream maker's instructions. Store the finished ice cream in the chilled container.

Reach for this recipe in late spring to early summer when the honey and fresh lavender seasons overlap.

VIETNAMESE COFFEE
ICE CREAM

MAKES 1 QUART ∗ PREP TIME: 30 MINUTES, PLUS CHILLING AND FREEZING

If you've ever had the pleasure of drinking a Vietnamese iced coffee, you will love this ice cream. If you have not, you are in for a yummy surprise. *Ca phe da* is strongly brewed French roast coffee dripped into a glass containing sweetened condensed milk, stirred, then poured over ice. When the French brought coffee to Vietnam in the 1800s, there was very limited dairy available, so they used sweetened condensed milk instead. This ice cream has a lovely, soft, almost chewy texture.

¾ cup ground dark French roast coffee, divided

1½ cups boiling water, divided

1 (14-ounce) can sweetened condensed milk

¼ cup heavy (whipping) cream

PREP

Brew the coffee in two batches. We use a Melitta filter cone set over a measuring cup. Put half the ground coffee into a medium bowl and pour ¾ cup of boiling water over the grounds. Stir it just enough to moisten all the coffee, then pour this into the filter and let it drip until no more coffee comes from the filter. Discard the filter and grounds and repeat for the remaining ground coffee and water. This will give you about 1 cup of strong brewed coffee.

MAKE THE BASE

In a medium bowl, stir together the sweetened condensed milk and heavy cream. Stir in the brewed coffee and mix until completely smooth. Cover the bowl with plastic wrap and thoroughly chill the base in the refrigerator for at least 2 hours, or preferably overnight.

FREEZE

Place a 1-quart container with a tight-fitting lid in the freezer to chill. Freeze the chilled ice cream base according to your ice cream maker's instructions. Store the finished ice cream in the chilled container.

HONEY
FROZEN YOGURT

Quick, simple, and refreshing, this frozen yogurt pairs seamlessly with almost any fruit; we think it has a particular affinity for fresh strawberries. Different honeys, of course, have very different flavors. Experiment with various varietals to discover which flavors suit your tastes. Maybe there is a beekeeper in your neighborhood who is willing to trade frozen yogurt for local honey.

4 cups plain whole-milk French-style yogurt

¼ cup sugar

7 tablespoons honey

Few drops pure vanilla extract

MAKE THE BASE

In a medium bowl, mix the yogurt and sugar together. Stir in the honey until the mixture is smooth and no streaks of honey remain. Stir in the vanilla, taste for sweetness, and adjust if necessary. Cover the bowl with plastic wrap and thoroughly chill the base in the refrigerator for at least 2 hours, or preferably overnight.

FREEZE

Place a 1-quart container with a tight-fitting lid in the freezer to chill. Freeze the base according to your ice cream maker's instructions. Store the finished frozen yogurt in the chilled container.

 Honey does not spoil, so do not worry if it has been in your pantry for a while. If the honey is not very liquid, warm it over very low heat until it melts. This recipe can easily be scaled up for larger batches.

CHAPTER EIGHT

festive

Holidays and special occasions seem incomplete without a celebratory dessert to punctuate the revelry. Whatever the event, make a statement and rejoice with these sweet frozen delicacies, from refined dinner parties ending with Baked Alaska (page 153) to a summer barbecue and Watermelon Ice Pops (page 152). There are treats for every season and every special occasion in the recipes that follow, but we suppose you will want to enjoy them anytime of the year.

QUATRE ÉPICES
ICE CREAM

MAKES 2 QUARTS * PREP/COOK TIME: 1 HOUR, PLUS CHILLING AND FREEZING

Quatre épices is a French spice blend. Its name means "four spices," but we like to include one or two additions for good measure. The core four seasonings are black pepper, nutmeg, cinnamon, and cloves, and we like to include fresh ginger and allspice berries. The ice cream custard base is flavored initially with this blend of spices, then the frozen ice cream is finished with small amounts of the same ground spices, swirled throughout. This ice cream is great when the weather turns cold and damp, served alongside a slice of warm apple or pumpkin pie.

4 cups heavy (whipping) cream

½ cup sliced peeled ginger

2½ cups half-and-half

1⅓ cups sugar

1 (3-inch) cinnamon stick

3 whole cloves

3 allspice berries

½ teaspoon black peppercorns

½ teaspoon freshly grated nutmeg

Generous pinch kosher salt

12 extra-large egg yolks

Generous pinch ground cinnamon (optional)

Generous pinch ground ginger (optional)

Generous pinch ground cloves (optional)

MAKE THE BASE

Fill a large heat-proof bowl halfway with ice. Nestle a smaller heat-proof bowl in the ice and place a fine-mesh strainer over it. Add the heavy cream to the smaller of the chilled bowls. Set aside.

In a small saucepan of boiling water, blanch the ginger slices for 3 minutes. Drain.

In a heavy bottomed, 4-quart pot over medium-low heat, combine the half-and-half, sugar, cinnamon stick, cloves, allspice berries, peppercorns, nutmeg, salt, and blanched ginger. Heat the mixture, stirring occasionally with a heat-proof spatula to dissolve the sugar, until it is steamy and hot. Do not allow the mixture to boil. Remove the pot from the heat, cover, and set aside to steep. After 30 minutes, taste the base for the spice level. It should be aromatic and noticeably spiced. If it seems mild, allow it to steep for another 30 minutes.

In a small heat-proof bowl, whisk the egg yolks to combine.

Return the pot to the stove and reheat the ice cream base over medium-low heat. When the liquid is hot, temper the egg yolks by pouring 1 cup of the hot liquid into the egg yolks in a slow, steady stream, whisking constantly. Immediately pour the tempered yolks into the pot, whisking constantly to combine. Scrape out the bowl that contained the egg yolks, using a heat-proof spatula.

Lower the heat under the pot slightly, and use the spatula to stir and scrape the bottom of the pot to keep the yolks from scrambling. Continue to gently cook the custard base, stirring constantly and adjusting the heat if necessary, until the base begins to thicken and evenly coats the spatula. This should take about 5 minutes.

Strain the base into the chilled heavy cream. Do not scrape out the pot. Stir the mixture to stop the cooking process. If you desire, stir in some or all of the strained-out spices. Thoroughly chill the base over the ice, or cover the bowl with plastic wrap and refrigerate for at least 2 hours, or preferably overnight.

FREEZE

Place a 2-quart container with a tight-fitting lid in the freezer to chill. Before freezing the ice cream base, strain out any remaining whole spices. Freeze the base according to your ice cream maker's instructions. Swirl the ground cinnamon (if using), ground ginger (if using), and ground cloves (if using) into the finished ice cream for a speckled effect. Store in the chilled container.

WATERMELON
ICE POPS

MAKES 6 TO 8 POPS * PREP TIME: 10 MINUTES, PLUS FREEZING

Say what you will about strawberries and peaches being the embodiment of summertime, but who can argue with juicy watermelon as the official mascot of those lazy days? Refreshingly cold, with natural sun-drenched sweetness, watermelon is the go-to flavor for ice pops.

3½ cups large (2-inch) watermelon cubes

½ cup sugar, plus more to taste

2 teaspoons freshly squeezed lemon juice, plus more to taste

Generous pinch kosher salt

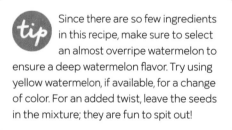

tip Since there are so few ingredients in this recipe, make sure to select an almost overripe watermelon to ensure a deep watermelon flavor. Try using yellow watermelon, if available, for a change of color. For an added twist, leave the seeds in the mixture; they are fun to spit out!

PREP

Freeze your ice pop molds according to the manufacturer's instructions.

MAKE THE BASE

Purée the watermelon in a food processor or blender. Pass the purée though a medium-mesh strainer into a small bowl. Stir in the sugar, lemon juice, and salt until the sugar and salt are dissolved completely. You should have about $2\frac{1}{2}$ cups of purée. Taste the purée and adjust the sweetness with a bit more sugar or a few more drops of lemon juice if necessary. Note that the mixture should be very sweet, as the sweetness will be somewhat diluted when frozen.

FREEZE

Fill the chilled ice pop molds with the purée, and freeze.

BAKED ALASKA

MAKES 8 SERVINGS ✳ PREP TIME: 2 HOURS, PLUS CHILLING
COOK TIME: 12 TO 17 MINUTES FOR THE TART SHELLS AND
2 TO 3 MINUTES FOR THE COMPLETED BAKED ALASKA

We reserve this impressive dessert for special occasions and honored guests. Presumably, the Alaska in baked Alaska refers to the snow-white peaks of meringue atop frozen ice cream. We nestle ice cream (sometimes we use two flavors, or even sherbet!) inside a buttery pastry dough shell then seal it with whipped meringue. It's then flash-baked in a 500°F oven until the meringue peaks brown. Baked Alaska is delicious alone or with Strawberry Sauce (page 209). It's the very definition of a showstopper.

FOR THE TART DOUGH

2 cups plus 1 tablespoon unsalted butter, at room temperature

¾ cup sugar

Generous pinch kosher salt

3 extra-large egg yolks

1 teaspoon pure vanilla extract

1¾ cups all-purpose flour, sifted

FOR THE BAKED ALASKA

1 tablespoon unsalted butter, melted

1 quart ice cream, any flavor of your choosing

1 quart sherbet, any flavor of your choosing (optional)

FOR THE MERINGUE

½ cup egg whites (about 3 extra-large), warmed slightly

1 teaspoon pure vanilla extract

¼ teaspoon cream of tartar

Generous pinch kosher salt

1 cup sugar >>

MAKE THE TART DOUGH

In the bowl of a standing electric mixer fitted with the paddle attachment, cream together the butter, sugar, and salt on medium-high speed until pale and fluffy, about 5 minutes. Reduce the mixer speed to its lowest setting and add the egg yolks and vanilla; continue mixing until combined. Stop the mixer, scrape down the sides of the bowl, then beat the mixture for another 30 seconds.

With the mixer still on the lowest speed, gradually add the flour and mix until the dough comes together in a single mass and no dry flour remains visible. If the dough seems overly dry, add a few drops of water, but this should not be necessary.

Wrap the dough tightly in plastic wrap and flatten it into a thin disc. Refrigerate it until very cold.

MAKE THE BAKED ALASKA

Remove the plastic wrap from the dough and place the dough on a sheet of parchment paper. Dust the dough with a little flour and place a second piece of parchment on top of it. Using a rolling pin, roll the dough to a thickness of $\frac{1}{16}$ inch. Transfer the parchment and dough to a baking sheet and refrigerate for 15 minutes.

Once the dough has chilled, remove the top sheet of parchment and use a cutter or wide-mouthed jar to stamp out 8 rounds of dough, each large enough to fit in a 4-inch fluted or straight-sided tartlet mold. Prick the dough rounds several times with the tines of a fork. Return the baking sheet to the refrigerator for a few minutes.

Brush the tartlet molds with the melted butter and place a round of dough in each mold. Let the dough warm for a minute and then evenly and gently press the dough into the molds. Fill in any holes with extra bits of dough and trim any excess dough from the edges. Place the tartlet molds in the freezer.

Preheat the oven to 350°F.

Remove the tartlet shells from the freezer and place them on a baking sheet. Bake until they are lightly golden and fully baked, 12 to 17 minutes. Remove from the oven and allow to cool completely.

Carefully scoop a portion of ice cream into each cooled tartlet shell and top each scoop with a smaller scoop of the sherbet (if using). Flatten slightly with an offset spatula or a metal spoon. The bottom of a ramekin also works well. The ice cream and sherbet should fill the shell but not hang over the edges, as they will melt during baking. Return the baking sheet with the filled tartlet shells to the freezer for 2 to 3 hours, or overnight.

Preheat the oven to 500°F.

At this point, make the meringue according to the following instructions.

MAKE THE MERINGUE

In the bowl of a standing electric mixer fitted with the whisk attachment, whisk the egg whites on medium speed until foamy.

Add the vanilla, cream of tartar, and salt. Continue whisking until soft peaks form. Then slowly add the sugar in a continuous stream, whisking constantly. Beat the meringue until it is stiff and shiny and holds a peak.

Transfer the meringue to a pastry bag fitted with a star tip.

Gently remove the filled tartlet shells from their pans and place them on a baking sheet. Pipe a layer of whipped meringue over the ice cream in each tartlet so the ice cream is full encased within.

Bake the Alaskas until nicely browned, 2 to 3 minutes total. A few dark edges are okay and make for a nice presentation. You can also brown the tops using a kitchen blowtorch. Serve immediately.

WARM PANETTONE
STUFFED WITH ICE CREAM

SERVES 10 * PREP/COOK TIME: 30 MINUTES, PLUS FREEZING

1 large panettone

2 cups Crema Ice Cream (page 131),
Eggnog Ice Cream (page 165), or
Dark Chocolate Ice Cream (page 67)

Confectioners' sugar, for garnish (optional)

Cake and ice cream complement each other so well we thought of combining them into one luscious creation. Panettone is a magnificent Italian holiday tradition. Bakers begin preparing the bread during the weeks that lead up to Christmas. Part buttery cake, part yeasted bread, it is baked in a paper sleeve. Its interior is dotted with dried fruits and candied peel. For this dessert, we cut a hole in the bottom of the panettone, remove some filling, pack it with freshly churned ice cream, and reseal it. Then it's frozen overnight, flash-baked in the oven to warm the bread, and sliced for a portion of warm cake and cold ice cream. Enjoy with a glass of dessert wine.

Remove the paper sleeve from the sides and bottom of the panettone and discard. Using a small serrated knife, cut a circle through the bottom of the panettone, leaving a 2-inch border around the edge of the cake. Carefully remove the cut-away portion and reserve it. Trim away some of the interior portion of the cake, creating a deep cavity in the panettone, large enough to hold 2 cups of ice cream. Be careful to leave at least 2 inches of cake on all sides, including the top.

Fill the cavity with the ice cream, preferably freshly made ice cream right from the machine. Smooth the ice cream with a spoon and close the cavity with the cutaway bottom of panettone to seal the ice cream in the cake. Wrap the whole cake tightly in plastic wrap and place it in the freezer, cut-side up. Freeze overnight.

Preheat the oven to 375°F.

Remove the panettone from the freezer and place it on a parchment paper–lined baking sheet. Place the sheet in the oven for 5 to 7 minutes.

Place the warm panettone on a wooden cutting board. Dust the top of the cake with confectioners' sugar (if using). Use a sharp knife to cut wedges of ice cream and cake and serve.

 You can find panettone in most supermarkets, gourmet shops, Italian bakeries, or online retailers after Thanksgiving and through the New Year holiday. We prefer imported Italian brands as they are made in a traditional manner.

CASSATA

SERVES 8 TO 12 * PREP/COOK TIME: 1 HOUR, PLUS FREEZING

This is a version of the famous Sicilian dessert, in frozen form. Studded with bits of chocolate, candied citrus peel, and pistachios, it is as beautiful as it is delicious. You don't even need an ice cream maker for this one. It can be molded into a loaf pan, frozen, and sliced or scooped easily, making this a versatile component to more complex desserts if you are feeling ambitious.

tip To combine this with ice cream or a layer of soaked sponge cake, make half the recipe. In the bottom of the lined loaf pan, place a liqueur-soaked piece of sponge cake, fitting it in tightly, or 2 cups of a complementary ice cream flavor, spread evenly in the bottom of the loaf pan. Then add the cassata on top of it.

Canola oil

¾ cup sugar

6 tablespoons water

1 tablespoon corn syrup

½ cup egg whites (about 3 extra-large)

1¼ cups heavy (whipping) cream

¼ cup coarsely grated or chopped bittersweet or semisweet chocolate

¼ cup chopped candied orange or tangerine peel

¼ cup chopped pistachios

3 to 4 tablespoons orange liqueur, such as Grand Marnier

Brush the interior of a 6-cup loaf pan with a thin layer of oil. Line the pan with plastic wrap, leaving a 2-inch border of wrap overhanging all sides of the pan. Smooth out the wrinkles in the plastic and push the wrap neatly into the corners. Place the pan in the freezer.

In a small, heavy-bottomed pot over medium heat, combine the sugar, water, and corn syrup. Clip a candy thermometer to the edge of the pot (make sure it is submerged, but don't let the tip touch the bottom of the pot). Bring the syrup to a simmer. >>

In the bowl of a standing mixer fitted with the whisk attachment, whisk the egg whites on medium-high speed until they form soft peaks.

Bring the simmering syrup to a boil and cook until the thermometer reads 240°F. Remove the pot from the heat.

Turn down the mixer speed to medium-low and add the hot syrup to the egg whites in a slow, steady stream. Increase the speed to medium and let the whites and syrup beat until the meringue becomes glossy and holds its shape. Reduce the speed to the lowest setting and continue to mix until the meringue has cooled, 3 to 5 minutes. This keeps the meringue at the texture you want without overbeating it.

While the meringue is cooling, pour the heavy cream into a large stainless-steel bowl and whisk it into soft peaks, ideally the same texture as the meringue. Add the meringue to the whipped cream and carefully fold them together until just combined. Fold in the chocolate until just combined, followed by the candied peel and then the pistachios. Finally, fold in the orange liqueur. Pour the mixture into the chilled loaf pan and fold the extra plastic wrap over the top of the mixture. Freeze the cassata for 4 to 6 hours, or overnight.

To serve, chill a serving platter. Unwrap the plastic from the top of the cassata. Briefly dip the bottom and sides of the loaf pan in cold water and invert the pan onto the chilled platter. Gently pull the edges of the plastic wrap to pull the cassata out of the pan and onto the platter. Remove the plastic and discard. Serve the cassata, using a knife to slice portions.

 To keep from overfolding the meringue and compromising its texture, briefly folding in the ingredients one at a time is an important step. Once you add the final flavoring, the ingredients will be fully incorporated and the mixture will retain its soft peaks. Putting the bowl over a container of ice while folding is helpful, too.

SUMMER SUNSET
BOMBE

SERVES 12 * PREP TIME: 20 MINUTES, PLUS FREEZING

This preparation combines three distinct, seasonal flavors in one visually stunning dessert. Create your own combinations of complementary flavors, with one caveat: It's best to surround a sherbet with two ice creams for balance. This trio reminds us that the days are getting longer and pastoral summer sunsets lie ahead.

Canola oil

1 quart Toasted Almond Ice Cream (page 43)

1 quart Apricot Sherbet (page 102)

1 quart Plum Ice Cream (page 104)

Ladyfingers or sponge cake (optional)

Kirschwasser, for soaking (optional)

Strawberry Sauce (page 209),
    for garnish (optional)

Chopped Candied Nuts (page 203),
    for garnish (optional)

Brush the interior of two $8\frac{1}{2}$-by-$4\frac{1}{2}$-inch loaf pans with canola oil. Line the pans with plastic wrap, leaving a 2-inch border of wrap overhanging all sides of the pans. Smooth out the wrinkles and push the wrap neatly into the corners.

Layer the bottom third of each loaf pan with toasted almond ice cream. Smooth the layer with an offset spatula or the back of a spoon. Place the loaf pans in the freezer for at least 2 hours.

Layer the middle third of each loaf pan with apricot sherbet. Smooth the layer with an offset spatula or the back of a spoon. Place the loaf pans in the freezer for another 2 hours.

Fill the rest of the loaf pans with plum ice cream. Smooth the top with an offset spatula or the back of a spoon. Give each loaf pan two or three raps on the countertop to compact the ice cream and force out any trapped air pockets. >>

Trim the ladyfingers (if using) to fit neatly in the loaf pan and gently press them into the plum ice cream layer. Soak the ladyfingers with the Kirschwasser (if using) to keep them from freezing.

Fold the excess plastic wrap over the top of the loaf pans to completely cover the bombes. Freeze them overnight.

To serve, unwrap the plastic from the top of the bombes and invert each bombe onto a wooden cutting board. The ladyfinger layer (if used) is now on the bottom. Remove the

loaf pan and discard the plastic wrap. Cut thick slices of the bombes to serve. If you wish, garnish the servings with strawberry sauce or chopped candied nuts.

tip Create new flavor marriages with winter fruits, chocolate variations, or berry combos. The possibilities are limitless.

CRISPY MERINGUE BOATS

MAKES ABOUT 20 BOATS ✳ PREP TIME: 30 MINUTES
COOK TIME: 1 HOUR TO 1 HOUR, 15 MINUTES

Here's a great use for all those unused egg whites. Stiffly whipped, then shaped and dried in the oven, what emerges is a wonderful vessel for a sundae. Line a boat with a generous dollop of whipped cream, top with a scoop or two of your favorite ice cream or sherbet, and garnish with anything from Chocolate Sauce (page 208) and nuts to fresh or Candied Fruit Chips (page 219).

⅓ cup egg whites (about 2 extra-large), at room temperature, free from any yolk bits

⅛ teaspoon cream of tartar

¾ cup confectioners' sugar

1½ teaspoons cornstarch

5 tablespoons granulated sugar

⅛ teaspoon pure vanilla extract

Generous pinch kosher salt

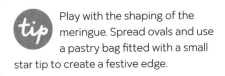

tip Play with the shaping of the meringue. Spread ovals and use a pastry bag fitted with a small star tip to create a festive edge.

Combine the egg whites and cream of tartar in the bowl of a standing electric mixer. Set the bowl over a pot of barely simmering water and use your clean, dry fingers to stir the mixture until it reaches body temperature. Set aside.

Sift the confectioners' sugar and cornstarch together into a small bowl. Set aside.

In the standing mixer fitted with the whisk attachment, beat the warm egg whites on medium speed until they begin to foam. Gradually add the granulated sugar and continue to whisk the egg whites until they become shiny and very thick, about 5 minutes.

Turn off the mixer and add the powdered sugar and cornstarch. Turn the mixer speed to medium-high and whisk until the meringue is stiff but not dry, about 5 minutes. Whisk in the vanilla and salt. The meringue should be stiff but not dry, creamy, and glossy.

Preheat the oven to 225°F. Line two baking sheets with parchment paper.

With a 1-ounce ice cream scoop or large soup spoon, portion the meringue onto the baking sheets, leaving room between each portion to spread them out a bit without >>

touching. Additionally, form 2–3 small meringue boats, about 1-inch wide. You will use these small boats to test the meringue for doneness. Using the back of a spoon or a small offset spatula, shape the meringue portions to form small boats, starting in the middle and spreading outward in a circle, leaving a raised edge around the outside and a bowl in the middle. Try not to let the bottom get too thin in the middle, as the baked boats are fragile and may break after drying.

Bake the meringues for 1 hour.

Remove a baking sheet from the oven and use scissors to carefully cut one of the 1-inch tester meringues from the parchment sheet; set it aside. Return the baking sheet to the oven.

When the meringue is cool, check it for doneness. It should snap in half and be crispy when bitten into. If not, continue baking the meringues still in the oven for another 10 or 15 minutes, then test another meringue. If the meringue is done, remove the baking sheets from the oven and let the boats cool completely.

Store the cooled meringue boats in an air-tight container for up to 2 weeks.

 We prefer to whip meringue on medium to medium-high speed. This gives the sugar a chance to dissolve and allows you to monitor the stiffness of the meringue more easily. Too high a speed may result in over-beaten meringue.

EGGNOG
ICE CREAM

MAKES 2 QUARTS * PREP/COOK TIME: 2 TO 3 HOURS, PLUS CHILLING AND FREEZING

Most time-honored recipes for eggnog call for spices such as cinnamon, nutmeg, and vanilla, and a kick of booze. We wanted our holiday ice cream social to ring a bit louder, so we punched up the traditional custard with ginger and orange peel. A long steep is the key to coaxing out all of the flavors in the base. Make certain your spices are fresh, as their strength diminishes with age.

1½ cups half-and-half

1 cup sugar

1 Madagascar vanilla bean, split lengthwise and seeds scraped out

1 (3-inch) cinnamon stick

5 whole cloves

4 allspice berries

1½ star anise pods

4 wide strips fresh orange peel

½ teaspoon freshly grated nutmeg

½ teaspoon ground ginger

3 cups heavy (whipping) cream

8 extra-large egg yolks

2 to 4 tablespoons brandy, rum, or bourbon

MAKE THE BASE

In a heavy-bottomed 2-quart pot over medium heat, combine the half-and-half and sugar. Bring the mixture just to the boiling point, stirring occasionally to dissolve the sugar, then turn off the heat. Stir in the vanilla bean seeds and pod, cinnamon, cloves, allspice, star anise, orange peel, nutmeg, and ginger. Remove the pot from the heat, cover it, and set aside for 20 minutes to steep.

Reheat the mixture over medium-low heat. Once it is hot, turn off the heat, cover the pot, and let the spices steep for 1 hour. Taste the steeped mixture. It should be strong flavored (remember you will be adding more sugar, egg yolks, and heavy cream). If you prefer a stronger flavor, simply reheat the mixture and steep it a little longer. Then taste the steeping mixture. If it is nice and strong, you can begin to make the custard.

Fill a large heat-proof bowl halfway with ice. Nestle a smaller heat-proof bowl in the ice and place a fine-mesh strainer over it. Add the heavy cream to the smaller of the chilled bowls. Set aside.

In a small heat-proof bowl, whisk the egg yolks to combine. Set aside. >>

When you have achieved your preferred flavor of the base, return the pot to the stove and reheat the mixture over medium-low heat. When the liquid is hot, temper the egg yolks by pouring 1 cup of the hot liquid into the egg yolks in a slow, steady stream, whisking constantly. Immediately pour the tempered yolks into the pot, whisking constantly to combine. Scrape out the bowl that contained the egg yolks, using a heat-proof spatula.

Lower the heat under the pot slightly, and use the spatula to stir and scrape the bottom of the pot to keep the yolks from scrambling. Continue to gently cook the custard base, stirring constantly and adjusting the heat if necessary, until the base begins to thicken and evenly coats the spatula. This should take about 5 minutes.

Strain the custard into the chilled heavy cream. Do not scrape out the pot. Stir the mixture to stop the cooking process and to combine the custard and cream. Thoroughly chill the base over the ice, or cover the bowl with plastic wrap and refrigerate for at least 2 hours, or preferably overnight.

FREEZE

Place a 2-quart container with a tight-fitting lid in the freezer to chill. Right before freezing the ice cream base, stir in 2 tablespoons of brandy. Taste the base and add up to 2 more tablespoons of brandy, if desired. Freeze the base according to your ice cream maker's instructions. Store the finished ice cream in the chilled container.

tip For a few festive flecks in your frozen eggnog, stir in a pinch of ground cinnamon along with the booze before freezing the ice cream. Surprisingly, or not, this ice cream pairs well with Chocolate Sauce (page 208) and Creamy Caramel Sauce (page 201), and would also make a delicious holiday *affogato*!

PRICKLY PEAR
ICE POPS

MAKES 6 ICE POPS * PREP/COOK TIME: 10 MINUTES, PLUS CHILLING AND FREEZING

The prickly pear goes by many names: cactus fruit, Indian fig, or, in Spanish, *tuna*. The skin is inedible and is covered in cactus-like spines, which are usually removed by the time they reach market, for convenient handling. When the interior seeds and flesh are puréed, it yields a vibrant, fuchsia-colored juice that makes a stunning and delicious ice pop.

1 cup water

1 cup sugar

Generous pinch kosher salt

4 prickly pears

2 teaspoons freshly squeezed lemon juice

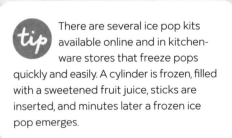

There are several ice pop kits available online and in kitchenware stores that freeze pops quickly and easily. A cylinder is frozen, filled with a sweetened fruit juice, sticks are inserted, and minutes later a frozen ice pop emerges.

PREP

Freeze your ice pop molds according to the manufacturer's instructions.

MAKE THE BASE

In a small saucepan over high heat, combine the water, sugar, and salt. Stir the syrup until the sugar is dissolved. Set aside to cool slightly.

Peel the prickly pears and discard the skins. Place the flesh and seeds in a blender or food processor along with the lemon juice and syrup, and purée. Strain the purée through a medium-mesh strainer into a small bowl. Cover the bowl with plastic wrap and refrigerate to chill the mixture thoroughly.

FREEZE

Fill the ice pop molds with the chilled purée, and freeze.

HIBISCUS
ICE MILK

MAKES 1 QUART * PREP/COOK TIME: 15 MINUTES, PLUS CHILLING AND FREEZING

The hibiscus flower—known as *flor de Jamaica* in Mexico, where it is considered a delicacy—is a deep reddish-purple, vitamin-rich, dried blossom. Famously steeped and made into a tea that can be enjoyed either hot or cold, it has numerous health benefits. A bit sour, a touch sweet, it lends its unique flavor to this frozen ice milk for a surprising floral dessert. Look for dried hibiscus in Mexican groceries or tea shops, where it is sold loose and in bulk.

4 cups whole milk

¾ cup sugar, plus 2 tablespoons, divided

1½ cups dried hibiscus flowers

3 egg whites, at room temperature

Generous pinch kosher salt

PREP

Fill a large heat-proof bowl halfway with ice. Nestle a smaller heat-proof bowl in the ice and place a fine-mesh strainer over it. Set aside.

In a heavy-bottomed 2-quart saucepot over medium-low heat, combine the milk and ¾ cup of sugar. Heat the milk, stirring occasionally with a heat-proof spatula to dissolve the sugar, until it is steamy and hot. Do not let the mixture boil. When the sugar has dissolved and the milk is hot, stir in the flowers. Remove the pot from the heat, cover, and let the flowers steep for 5 minutes.

Strain the steeped milk into the chilled bowl setup. Avoid pressing on the steeped flowers, as they will be quite sour. Don't worry if some of the milk has curdled, it will adhere to the blossoms and be strained away. Discard the flowers.

MAKE THE BASE

While the milk chills, whisk the egg whites to stiff peaks either by hand or in a standing electric mixer fitted with the whisk attachment. When the whites begin to hold soft peaks, whisk in the salt. Gradually add 1 tablespoon of sugar, and continue to whisk. Add the remaining tablespoon of sugar and continue to whisk the egg whites until they are shiny and stiff.

Using a spatula, fold the egg whites into the chilled milk. Thoroughly chill the base over the ice, or cover the bowl with plastic wrap and refrigerate for at least 2 hours, or preferably overnight.

FREEZE

Place a 1-quart container with a tight-fitting lid in the freezer to chill. Freeze the ice milk base according to your ice cream maker's instructions. Store the finished ice milk in the chilled container.

 Cooking tip: Egg whites hold more volume (air) when they are at room temperature or slightly warm; this can quickly be achieved by placing them in a stainless-steel bowl and setting the bowl in a larger bowl of very warm water. They should feel warm to the touch, meaning they are at least 100°F.

PINK LEMON
GRANITA

MAKES 1 QUART * PREP/COOK TIME: 10 MINUTES, PLUS FREEZING

Believe it or not, (real) pink lemonade is made from pink lemons, commonly known as variegated lemons. Their skins are beautifully striated, with streaks of green; this lemon varietal is popular with home growers. Pink lemons are small, juicy, and thin-skinned, with pale pink flesh. The season is short for this rare citrus, which makes the juice highly prized. Here we make them into a simple, icy granita to showcase their pink hue and bright flavor. If pink lemons aren't available, try this recipe with regular old lemons. It will still be delicious.

2 cups water

1 cup sugar, or more to taste

Generous pinch kosher salt

1½ cups freshly squeezed pink lemon juice

PREP

Place an 8-by-12-inch glass or metal baking pan in the freezer to chill. The pan should rest flat on an easily accessible spot.

MAKE THE BASE

In a small, heavy saucepan over medium heat, combine the water, sugar, and salt. Stir often with a heat-proof spatula, and when the sugar is fully dissolved, remove the pan from the heat and set aside to cool.

Stir the lemon juice into the room-temperature syrup. Taste the granita and, if needed, adjust it for sweetness by stirring in more sugar, 1 teaspoon at a time.

FREEZE

Remove the chilled baking pan from the freezer and pour in the liquid. Return the pan to the freezer. After 30 minutes, use a fork to stir the granita from the outside in, stirring any ice crystals back into the liquid. Return the pan to the freezer. Repeat this step every 30 minutes for at least 3 hours, or until the entire mixture has frozen and has a uniformly light, "dry," crystalline texture. When the granita has reached this stage, cover it tightly with plastic wrap until you are ready to serve.

TUTTI-FRUTTI
ICE CREAM

MAKES 2 QUARTS * PREP/COOK TIME: 1 HOUR, PLUS CHILLING AND FREEZING

A gentleman who had an ice cream business in Okolona, Kentucky, created this flavor and named it after his daughter, Toodie. There are dozens of versions of this whimsical ice cream, each a bit different. This is our take on this festive flavor, but we also encourage you to create your own! Experiment and use those last little bits of dried fruits and nuts you have on hand in your cupboard—anything goes.

3 cups heavy (whipping) cream

8 extra-large egg yolks

1½ cups half-and-half

1 cup sugar

Zest of ½ orange

Generous pinch kosher salt

¼ cup sliced unblanched almonds

¼ cup walnuts

¼ cup dried cherries

¼ cup raisins or dried currants

¼ cup chopped candied pineapple

¼ cup chopped dried apricots

MAKE THE BASE

Fill a large heat-proof bowl halfway with ice. Nestle a smaller heat-proof bowl in the ice and place a fine-mesh strainer over it. Add the heavy cream to the smaller of the chilled bowls. Set aside.

In a small heat-proof bowl, whisk the egg yolks to combine. Set aside.

In a heavy-bottomed 4-quart pot over medium heat, combine the half-and-half, sugar, and zest. Heat the mixture, stirring occasionally with a heat-proof spatula to dissolve the sugar, until it is steamy and hot. Do not allow the mixture to boil.

When the liquid is hot, temper the egg yolks by pouring 1 cup of the liquid into the egg yolks in a slow, steady stream, whisking constantly. Immediately pour the tempered yolks into the pot, whisking constantly to combine. Scrape out the bowl that contained the egg yolks, using a heat-proof spatula.

Lower the heat under the pot slightly, and use the spatula to stir and scrape the bottom of the pot to keep the yolks from scrambling. Continue to gently cook the custard base, stirring constantly and adjusting the heat if necessary, until the base begins to thicken and evenly coats the spatula. This should take about 5 minutes.

Strain the custard into the chilled cream. Stir the mixture to stop the cooking process and to combine the custard and cream. Thoroughly chill the base over the ice, or cover the bowl with plastic wrap and refrigerate for at least 2 hours, or preferably overnight.

FREEZE

Place a 2-quart container with a tight-fitting lid in the freezer ito chill. Freeze the chilled ice cream base according to your ice cream maker's instructions.

TOAST THE NUTS

While the base is freezing, toast the nuts. Preheat the oven to 350°F. Place the almonds on one half of a baking sheet and the walnuts on the other half, all

in a single layer. Toast the nuts for 12 to 14 minutes. Allow the nuts to cool enough for the walnuts to be handled.

Rub the cooled walnuts between your fingers to loosen any skin that remains on the nuts. Coarsely chop the walnuts. Leave the sliced almonds whole. In a small bowl, combine the dried cherries, raisins, candied pineapple, dried apricots, and toasted nuts and toss them all together evenly.

Fold the dried fruit and toasted nut mixture into the finished ice cream as you are filling the chilled storage container.

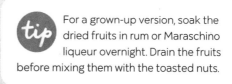

tip For a grown-up version, soak the dried fruits in rum or Maraschino liqueur overnight. Drain the fruits before mixing them with the toasted nuts.

boozy

Wine and distilled spirits are a magnificent addition to frozen concoctions for several reasons. Alcohol has a significantly lower freezing point than the main ingredients in custard, sherbet, and granita, which results in a slightly supple texture in the finished frozen concoction. Additionally, the complex, concentrated flavors offered by the likes of bourbon, brandy, red wine, and sake are compounded when blended with sweet creams and complementary fruits. While some high-end bottles may be costly, only a small amount finds its way into each recipe, thus offsetting the expense with multiple gatherings.

RUM-RAISIN
ICE CREAM

MAKES 2 QUARTS * PREP/COOK TIME: 30 MINUTES,
PLUS 1 DAY TO SOAK THE RAISINS, PLUS CHILLING AND FREEZING

This iconic flavor pairing reminds us of the delicious comfort and richness that a well-made bread pudding delivers. Rum-plumped sultana raisins meet and mingle with rich custard, creating a balanced ice cream—and a timeless adult favorite. We prefer to use aged rum, not too dark or too spicy, at an affordable price.

2 cups raisins

½ cup aged rum, such as Flor de Caña

4 cups heavy (whipping) cream

12 extra-large egg yolks

2½ cups half-and-half

1⅓ cups sugar

Generous pinch kosher salt

1 Madagascar vanilla bean, split lengthwise and seeds scraped out (optional)

PREP

The day before making the ice cream, place the raisins in a jar with the rum. Seal the jar and give it a good shake. Let the raisins soak for 24 hours or longer.

MAKE THE BASE

Fill a large heat-proof bowl halfway with ice. Nestle a smaller heat-proof bowl in the ice and place a fine-mesh strainer over it. Add the heavy cream to the smaller of the chilled bowls. Set aside.

In a small heat-proof bowl, whisk the egg yolks to combine. Set aside.

In a heavy-bottomed 4-quart pot over medium-low heat, combine the half-and-half, sugar, salt, and vanilla bean seeds and pod (if using). Heat the mixture, stirring occasionally with a heat-proof spatula to dissolve the sugar and salt, until it is steamy and hot. Do not allow the mixture to boil.

When the liquid is hot, temper the egg yolks by pouring 1 cup of the hot liquid into the egg yolks in a slow, steady stream, whisking constantly. Immediately pour the tempered yolks into the pot, whisking constantly to combine. Scrape out the bowl that contained the egg yolks, using a heat-proof spatula.

Lower the heat under the pot slightly, and use the spatula to stir and scrape the bottom of the pot to keep the yolks from scrambling. Continue to gently cook the custard base, stirring constantly and adjusting the heat if necessary, until the base begins to thicken and evenly coats the spatula. This should take about 5 minutes.

Strain the custard into the chilled heavy cream. Do not scrape out the saucepot. Stir the mixture to stop the cooking process and to combine the custard and cream. If you desire, add the strained-out vanilla pod to the base. Thoroughly chill the base over the ice, or cover the bowl with plastic wrap and refrigerate for at least 2 hours, or preferably overnight.

Place a 2-quart container with a tight-fitting lid in the freezer to chill.

Strain the rum off the raisins and reserve it. Roughly chop the raisins and set aside.

Stir the reserved rum into the chilled ice cream base. Remove the vanilla pod (if still in the base) and give the base a taste. Adjust the flavor with more rum if needed.

FREEZE

Freeze the chilled ice cream base according to your ice cream maker's instructions. Fold the raisins into the finished ice cream as you are filling the chilled container.

BOURBON-PECAN
ICE CREAM

MAKES 2 QUARTS * PREP/COOK TIME: 30 MINUTES, PLUS CHILLING AND FREEZING

Bourbon is as American as it gets, and no country seems to love pecans more than we do. Pecans are a Southern pantry staple, and embellishing ice cream laced with this high-octane corn liquor from the great state of Kentucky—you'll stand up and salute the flag. Seek out wild, organic pecans, which are smaller and tastier than the common supermarket nut. The Missouri Northern Pecan Growers has an online store, making direct ordering a cinch.

2 cups pecans

4 cups heavy (whipping) cream

12 extra-large egg yolks

2½ cups half-and-half

1⅓ cups sugar

Generous pinch kosher salt

1 Madagascar vanilla bean, split lengthwise and seeds scraped out (optional)

¼ to ½ cup bourbon

PREP

Preheat the oven to 350°F.

Spread the pecans in a single layer on a baking sheet and toast them until they are fragrant and lightly browned, 12 to 14 minutes. Let the pecans cool before roughly chopping them into small pieces.

MAKE THE BASE

Fill a large heat-proof bowl halfway with ice. Nestle a smaller heat-proof bowl in the ice and place a fine-mesh strainer over it. Add the heavy cream to the smaller of the chilled bowls. Set aside.

In a small heat-proof bowl, whisk the egg yolks to combine. Set aside.

In a heavy-bottomed 4-quart pot over medium-low heat, combine the half-and-half, sugar, salt, and vanilla bean seeds and pod (if using). Heat the mixture, stirring occasionally with a heat-proof spatula to dissolve the sugar and salt, until it is steamy and hot. Do not allow the mixture to boil. >>

When the liquid is hot, temper the egg yolks by pouring 1 cup of the hot liquid into the egg yolks in a slow, steady stream, whisking constantly. Immediately pour the tempered yolks into the pot, whisking constantly to combine. Scrape out the bowl that contained the egg yolks, using a heat-proof spatula.

Lower the heat under the pot slightly, and use the spatula to stir and scrape the bottom of the pot to keep the yolks from scrambling. Continue to gently cook the custard base, stirring constantly and adjusting the heat if necessary, until the base begins to thicken and evenly coats the spatula. This should take about 5 minutes.

Strain the custard into the chilled heavy cream. Do not scrape out the saucepot. Stir the mixture to stop the cooking process and to combine the custard and cream. If you desire, add the strained-out vanilla pod to the base. Thoroughly chill the base over the ice, or cover the bowl with plastic wrap and refrigerate for at least 2 hours, or preferably overnight.

Place a 2-quart container with a tight-fitting lid in the freezer to chill.

Stir $\frac{1}{4}$ cup of bourbon into the chilled ice cream base. Remove the vanilla pod (if still in the base) and give the base a taste. Adjust the flavor with up to $\frac{1}{4}$ cup more bourbon, if needed.

FREEZE

Freeze the chilled ice cream base according to your ice cream maker's instructions. Fold the chopped pecans into the finished ice cream as you are filling the chilled storage container, and freeze again for at least 4 hours, or preferably overnight.

GRAPEFRUIT SHERBET
WITH CAMPARI AND CANDIED GRAPEFRUIT

MAKES 1½ QUARTS * PREP/COOK TIME: 20 MINUTES, PLUS CHILLING AND FREEZING

These flavors are by way of Italy, something enjoyed over a long and leisurely cocktail "hour." At the end of the day, Italians head to small bars and enjoy low-alcohol aperitifs alongside snacks. Popular choices are Campari and Aperol, fluorescent red, bitter spirits laced with herbs and citrus that stimulate the appetite. We love the double presence of grapefruit, frozen and candied in this recipe, though the booze-free sherbet is delightful on its own.

2 cups water, or more to taste

¾ cup corn syrup

1¾ cups sugar, or more to taste

Generous pinch kosher salt, or more to taste

6 cups freshly squeezed grapefruit juice, such as from Oro Blanco or Ruby Red grapefruit, strained

½ cup Campari or Aperol (optional)

Candied Grapefruit Slices (page 213)

MAKE THE BASE

In a 2-quart pot over medium-high heat, combine the water, corn syrup, sugar, and salt to a boil. Occasionally stir the syrup to completely dissolve the sugar. Remove the pot from the heat and set it aside to cool to room temperature.

In a large bowl, mix together the syrup and grapefruit juice. Taste the base and adjust it with more sugar, water, or salt, if needed. Cover the bowl with plastic wrap and refrigerate to chill the base thoroughly for at least 2 hours, or preferably overnight.

FREEZE

Place a 2-quart container with a tight-fitting lid in the freezer to chill. Freeze the chilled sherbet base according to your ice cream maker's instructions. Store the finished sherbet in the chilled container.

SERVE

To serve, place a scoop or two of sherbet in each dish and pour a generous splash of Campari over the top (if using). Garnish with a few candied grapefruit slices.

SHAKERATO
(WHIPPED FRUIT SLUSH)

SERVES 4 ✳ PREP TIME: 5 MINUTES

This is our take on the shaken, chilled Italian drink of the same name. We love it as a whipped, frozen fruit slush, spiked with a shot of high-proof alcohol. Traditionally, grappa was the spirit of choice, but take liberties and use rum or vodka if you like. Intensely flavored, acidic sherbets work best, and their flavors are enhanced by the alcohol.

2 cups Pineapple Sherbet (page 87) or Tangerine Sherbet (page 88)

¼ cup grappa, vodka, or rum, or more to taste

Chill four aperitif or dessert glasses in the freezer.

Scoop the sherbet into a large bowl. Pour the grappa over the sherbet and beat the sherbet with the back of a wooden spoon until is slushy and the alcohol is mixed in.

Divide the slush equally between the chilled glasses and serve immediately.

 tip Grappa is a high-proof distillate derived from the skins and seeds left over from the winemaking process. Bottles can be quite expensive; fortunately, a little goes a long way.

RED WINE-RASPBERRY
GRANITA

MAKES 2 QUARTS * PREP/COOK TIME: 45 MINUTES, PLUS FREEZING

Ripe, fresh raspberries have a subtle, fruity wine flavor, so pairing them with a bold red wine is a great complement. Freezing the mixture into a flaky ice makes for a refreshing treat at the end of a hearty meal. Choose a red wine that is fruity but not overly sweet, as the sugars in it intensify when it is reduced. The idea is to have balance and lightness to this refresher while also packing a fruity punch from the ripe raspberries.

1 (750-mL) bottle red wine, such as Zinfandel

1 cup Champagne or sparkling wine

1 pint raspberries

1½ cups cold water

1¾ cups sugar

Generous pinch kosher salt

PREP

Place an 8-by-12-inch glass or metal baking pan in the freezer to chill. The pan should rest on an easily accessible, level spot.

MAKE THE BASE

In a 2-quart pot over high heat, bring the red wine and Champagne to a boil. Boil until the wines have reduced by one-third of their original volume. Remove the pot from the heat and stir in the raspberries. Cover the pot and set it aside until the wine has cooled to room temperature.

In a small bowl, combine the water, sugar, and salt, stirring until the sugar is completely dissolved.

Pour the wine and steeped raspberries into a blender and purée until smooth. Strain the purée through a fine-mesh strainer into a medium bowl. Stir in the sugar syrup. >>

FREEZE

Remove the chilled baking pan from the freezer and pour in the liquid. Return the pan to the freezer. After 30 minutes, use a fork to stir the granita from the outside in, stirring any ice crystals back into the liquid. Return the pan to the freezer. Repeat this step every 30 minutes for at least 3 hours, or until the entire mixture has frozen and has a uniformly light, "dry," crystalline texture. When the granita has reached this stage, cover it tightly with plastic wrap until you are ready to serve.

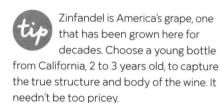

Zinfandel is America's grape, one that has been grown here for decades. Choose a young bottle from California, 2 to 3 years old, to capture the true structure and body of the wine. It needn't be too pricey.

APPLE BRANDY
ICE CREAM WITH SULTANAS

MAKES 2 QUARTS * PREP/COOK TIME: 30 MINUTES,
PLUS 1 DAY TO SOAK THE SULTANAS, PLUS CHILLING AND FREEZING

The central theme behind this ice cream is concentrated flavors; ripe apples, fortified high-proof brandy, and sweet sultana raisins. Apples, brandy, and raisins are a seamless combination, with each individual ingredient sharing notes with the other. We adore Calvados, the apple liqueur from the French region of the same name, but it is expensive. American distillers do a fine job making apple brandies, and a domestic bottle will fit your budget.

1 cup sultanas or golden raisins

¼ cup bonded 100-proof apple
    brandy or Calvados

4 cups heavy (whipping) cream

12 extra-large egg yolks

2½ cups half-and-half

1⅓ cups sugar

Generous pinch kosher salt

1 Madagascar vanilla bean, split lengthwise
    and seeds scraped out (optional)

PREP

The day before making the ice cream, place the sultanas in a jar with the apple brandy. Seal the jar and give it a good shake. Let the sultanas soak for 24 hours or longer.

MAKE THE BASE

Fill a large heat-proof bowl halfway with ice. Nestle a smaller heat-proof bowl in the ice and place a fine-mesh strainer over it. Add the heavy cream to the smaller of the chilled bowls. Set aside.

In a small heat-proof bowl, whisk the egg yolks to combine. Set aside.

In a heavy-bottomed 4-quart pot over medium-low heat, combine the half-and-half, sugar, salt, and vanilla bean seeds and pod (if using). Heat the mixture, stirring occasionally with a heat-proof spatula to dissolve the sugar and salt, until it is steamy and hot. Do not allow the mixture to boil.

When the liquid is hot, temper the egg yolks by pouring 1 cup of the liquid into the egg yolks in a slow, steady stream, whisking constantly. Immediately pour the tempered >>

yolks into the pot, whisking constantly to combine. Scrape out the bowl that contained the egg yolks, using a heat-proof spatula.

Lower the heat under the pot slightly, and use the spatula to stir and scrape the bottom of the pot to keep the yolks from scrambling. Continue to gently cook the custard base, stirring constantly and adjusting the heat if necessary, until the base begins to thicken and evenly coats the spatula. This should take about 5 minutes.

Strain the custard into the chilled heavy cream. Do not scrape out the saucepot. Stir the mixture to stop the cooking process and to combine the custard and cream. If you desire, add the strained-out vanilla pod to the base. Thoroughly chill the base over the ice, or cover the bowl with plastic wrap and refrigerate for at least 2 hours, or preferably overnight.

Place a 2-quart container with a tight-fitting lid in the freezer to chill.

Strain the brandy off the sultanas and reserve it. Roughly chop the sultanas and set aside.

Stir half of the reserved brandy into the chilled ice cream base. Remove the vanilla pod (if still in the base) and give the base a taste. Adjust the flavor with more brandy if needed.

FREEZE

Freeze the chilled ice cream base according to your ice cream maker's instructions. Fold the sultanas into the finished ice cream as you are filling the chilled container and freeze again for at least 4 hours, or preferably overnight.

 If you cannot find sultanas, raisins or even dried currants work great, too. The idea is that the concentrated fruit cuts the high proof of the alcohol and richness of the base.

FROZEN ZABAGLIONE

MAKES 4½ CUPS OR 1 LOAF PAN * PREP/COOK TIME: 30 MINUTES, PLUS FREEZING

Zabaglione (pronounced *za bal yo ne*), or *sabayon* in French, became famous as a mid-century dessert, usually prepared tableside. Pageantry and an open flame were on display in upscale dining establishments, as the maître d' would effortlessly whisk egg yolks and sugar with heady Marsala wine to airy ribbons. Ladled over fresh berries or stone fruit, it was a spectacle. In our rendition, we fold stiffly whipped cream into the finished zabaglione and then freeze the whole thing in a loaf pan, to be sliced and served like a traditional *semifreddo*.

Canola oil

4 extra-large egg yolks

½ cup sugar

Generous pinch kosher salt

⅔ cup Marsala wine, plus more for brushing

1 cup heavy (whipping) cream, chilled

6 ladyfingers (optional)

Fresh berries or Strawberry Sauce (page 209), for serving

Brush the interior of an 8½-by-4½-inch loaf pan with canola oil. Line the pan with plastic wrap, leaving a 3-inch border of wrap overhanging all sides of the pan. Smooth out the wrinkles and push the wrap neatly into the corners.

Fill a large heat-proof bowl halfway with ice and set it aside.

In a medium stainless-steel bowl, combine the egg yolks, sugar, and salt, whisking to combine. Gradually add the Marsala to the bowl, whisking to combine.

Set the bowl over a pot of gently simmering water. Continuously whisk the mixture until the yolks become pale and fluffy, about 15 minutes total. The zabaglione will nearly double in volume.

Transfer the bowl to the prepared ice bath and continue whisking the zabaglione until it is cool, about 5 minutes.

In a medium bowl, whip the chilled cream until it is firm and holds a peak. >>

Using a rubber spatula, gently but quickly fold half of the whipped cream into the zabaglione, being careful to maintain its volume, until no streaks remain. Fold in the remaining whipped cream, still taking care to retain the volume. Transfer the zabaglione to the loaf pan.

Gently line the top of the zabaglione with the ladyfingers (if using) and lightly brush them with a bit of Marsala to moisten them.

Lightly tap the pan on the counter 2 or 3 times to release any trapped air bubbles. Fold the plastic over the top of the zabaglione and freeze it for at least 5 hours, or preferably overnight.

When completely firm, peel the plastic away from the top of the zabaglione and gently pull the edges of the plastic wrap to lift the zabaglione out of the pan and onto a wooden cutting board. Discard the plastic wrap. Cut the zabaglione into 2-inch-thick slices and serve with fresh berries or strawberry sauce.

 Marsala is a fortified wine with an alcohol content around 15 percent. It is generally available in two varieties, dry or sweet. Experiment with either, though we prefer the sweet for this recipe.

ASIAN PEAR
SHERBET WITH SAKE

MAKES 2 QUARTS * PREP TIME: 15 MINUTES, PLUS CHILLING AND FREEZING

Highly prized in Asia, the Asian pear can be costly and, therefore, is reserved for honorable guests or given as gifts. Not quite suitable for cooking, Asian pears are perfect for turning into a complex sherbet. The thin skin can be pared away or left intact for a more rounded, mild pear flavor. We accentuate the sweetness by including a generous pour of sake in the base, which complements the dry notes inherent in the fruit. Seek out unfiltered sake if you can.

4 Asian pears

2 Bosc pears

2 tablespoons freshly squeezed lemon juice

1 cup plus 2 tablespoons sugar, or more to taste

6 tablespoons sake, or more to taste

Generous pinch kosher salt, or more to taste

 If you prefer a smoother purée, pass it through a fine-mesh strainer prior to freezing.

PREP

Peel (if you desire) and roughly chop the Asian pears, discarding the seeds and core. Peel and core the Bosc pears, then quarter them. Put the fruit in a food processor. Add the lemon juice and finely purée the mixture, stopping the machine once to scrape down the sides of the work bowl. You should have about $5\frac{1}{2}$ cups of purée.

MAKE THE BASE

Transfer the purée to a medium bowl and whisk in the sugar, stirring until it is dissolved. Stir in the sake and the salt. Taste the sherbet base and adjust the seasoning with more sugar, sake, or salt, if needed. Cover the bowl with plastic wrap and refrigerate to chill the base thoroughly for at least 2 hours, or preferably overnight.

FREEZE

Place a 2-quart container with a tight-fitting lid in the freezer to chill. Freeze the chilled sherbet base according to your ice cream maker's instructions. Store the finished sherbet in the chilled container.

LATE-HARVEST RIESLING
ICE CREAM

MAKES 2 QUARTS * PREP/COOK TIME: 30 MINUTES, PLUS CHILLING AND FREEZING

Late harvest grapes have been left on the vine longer, so that they begin to lose their moisture and the sugars concentrate, like a raisin. The result is a lovely, sweet, and complex flavor that can hold its own in ice cream. This is a perfect accompaniment to fresh, baked, or poached pears. Be sure to reserve a glass or two of the wine to enjoy with dessert.

3 cups heavy (whipping) cream

8 extra-large egg yolks

1½ cups half-and-half

1 cup sugar

Generous pinch kosher salt

1½ cups late-harvest Riesling wine

MAKE THE BASE

Fill a large heat-proof bowl halfway with ice. Nestle a smaller heat-proof bowl in the ice and place a fine-mesh strainer over it. Add the heavy cream to the smaller of the chilled bowls. Set aside.

In a small heat-proof bowl, whisk the egg yolks to combine. Set aside.

In a heavy-bottomed 4-quart pot over medium-low heat, combine the half-and-half, sugar, and salt. Heat the mixture, stirring occasionally with a heat-proof spatula to dissolve the sugar, until it is steamy and hot. Do not allow the mixture to boil.

When the liquid is hot, temper the egg yolks by pouring 1 cup of the hot liquid into the egg yolks in a slow, steady stream, whisking constantly. Immediately pour the tempered yolks into the pot, whisking constantly to combine. Scrape out the bowl that contained the egg yolks, using a heat-proof spatula.

Lower the heat under the pot slightly, and use the spatula to stir and scrape the bottom of the pot to keep the yolks from scrambling. Continue to gently cook the custard base, stirring constantly and adjusting the heat if necessary, until the base begins to thicken and evenly coats the spatula. This should take about 5 minutes.

Strain the custard into the chilled heavy cream. Do not scrape out the pot. Stir the mixture to stop the cooking process and to combine the custard and cream. If you desire, add the strained-out vanilla pod to the base. Thoroughly chill the base over the ice, or cover the bowl with plastic wrap and refrigerate for at least 2 hours, or preferably overnight.

FREEZE

Place a 2-quart container with a tight-fitting lid in the freezer to chill. Remove the vanilla pod (if still in the base), stir the wine into the chilled ice cream base, and freeze the base according to your ice cream maker's instructions. Store the finished ice cream in the chilled container.

 tip Alcohol ice creams tend to be on the softer side. This ice cream is best when made the day before and left to cure overnight in the freezer.

AMARETTO
ICE CREAM WITH DRIED CHERRIES

MAKES 2 QUARTS ✳ PREP/COOK TIME: 40 MINUTES,
PLUS 1 DAY TO SOAK THE CHERRIES, PLUS CHILLING AND FREEZING

Our friend and talented chef Ryan Childs reintroduced us to the pleasure of amaretto liqueur via his shaken amaretto sour cocktail. Then again, he hails from Portland, Oregon, where everything hip seems to originate these days. The traditional garnish for that easy-to-drink libation is a cherry, so like any first-rate bartender, we blend dried cherries into our amaretto-spiked ice cream. Cheers!

2 cups dried cherries

½ cup amaretto

12 extra-large egg yolks

4 cups heavy (whipping) cream

2½ cups half-and-half

1⅓ cups sugar

Generous pinch kosher salt

1 Madagascar vanilla bean, split lengthwise and seeds scraped out (optional)

PREP

The day before making the ice cream, place the cherries in a jar with the amaretto. Seal the jar and give it a good shake. Let the cherries soak for 24 hours or longer.

MAKE THE BASE

Fill a large heat-proof bowl halfway with ice. Nestle a smaller heat-proof bowl in the ice and place a fine-mesh strainer over it. Add the heavy cream to the smaller of the chilled bowls. Set aside.

In a small heat-proof bowl, whisk the egg yolks to combine. Set aside.

In a heavy-bottomed 4-quart pot over medium-low heat, combine the half-and-half, sugar, salt, and vanilla bean seeds and pod (if using). Heat the mixture, stirring occasionally with a heat-proof spatula to dissolve the sugar and salt, until it is steamy and hot. Do not allow the mixture to boil. >>

When the liquid is hot, temper the egg yolks by pouring 1 cup of the hot liquid into the egg yolks in a slow, steady stream, whisking constantly. Immediately pour the tempered yolks into the pot, whisking constantly to combine. Scrape out the bowl that contained the egg yolks, using a heat-proof spatula.

Lower the heat under the pot slightly, and use the spatula to stir and scrape the bottom of the pot to keep the yolks from scrambling. Continue to gently cook the custard base, stirring constantly and adjusting the heat if necessary, until the base begins to thicken and evenly coats the spatula. This should take about 5 minutes.

Strain the custard into the chilled heavy cream. Do not scrape out the saucepot. Stir the mixture to stop the cooking process and to combine the custard and cream. If you desire, add the strained-out vanilla pod to the base. Thoroughly chill the base over the ice, or cover the bowl with plastic wrap and refrigerate for at least 2 hours, or preferably overnight.

Place a 2-quart container with a tight-fitting lid in the freezer to chill.

Strain the amaretto off the cherries and reserve it. Pulse the fruit in a food processor or blender until it is chunky yet slightly puréed. Set aside.

Stir the reserved amaretto into the chilled ice cream base. Remove the vanilla pod (if still in the base) and give the base a taste. Adjust the flavor with more amaretto if needed.

FREEZE

Freeze the chilled ice cream base according to your ice cream maker's instructions. Swirl the chunky cherry purée through the finished ice cream as you are filling the chilled container and freeze again for at least 4 hours, or preferably overnight.

PIÑA COLADA
SHERBET

MAKES 1 QUART * PREP/COOK TIME: 15 MINUTES, PLUS CHILLING AND FREEZING

The head-for-the-beach flavors of pineapple and coconut along with a good shot of rum make this a delicious grown-up sherbet. Although you can omit the rum, it does add a lovely flavor and texture to the finished product. Serve this sherbet in a tall, chilled glass with a maraschino cherry garnish (or a paper umbrella) and you are on vacation!

1½ cups canned coconut milk

1¾ cups pineapple juice, or more to taste

½ cup sugar, or more to taste

¼ cup rum, or more to taste

Few drops pure vanilla extract

tip This sherbet pairs nicely with Toasted Coconut Ice Cream (page 93) and Warm Caramelized Pineapple with Rum (page 210).

PREP

In a small saucepan over low heat, gently warm the coconut milk, just until the liquid and fat are smooth and mixed thoroughly.

MAKE THE BASE

Transfer the warm coconut milk to a medium bowl and add the pineapple juice and sugar, stirring until the sugar is dissolved. Add the rum and vanilla and mix well. Cover the bowl with plastic wrap and thoroughly chill the base in the refrigerator for at least 2 hours, or preferably overnight.

FREEZE

Place a 1-quart container with a tight-fitting lid in your freezer to chill. Give the chilled sherbet base a stir and taste, adjusting it with a little more pineapple juice, sugar, or rum, if needed. Freeze the base according to your ice cream maker's instructions. Store the finished sherbet in the chilled container.

CHAMPAGNE-ROSE
GRANITA

MAKES 2 QUARTS * PREP TIME: 20 MINUTES, PLUS FREEZING

If you want to impress your guests with a simple yet refined dessert, try this granita. Fresh rose petals are suspended in champagne ice and enhanced by floral rose syrup. Choose a dry Champagne or sparkling wine here since there is a good deal of sweetness in this recipe already. You are looking for a winey, bubbly kick and a floral, rosy ending—elegant indeed.

2⅔ cups water

¾ cup sugar

Generous pinch kosher salt

¾ teaspoon rose syrup (optional)

1 (750-mL) bottle Champagne or sparkling wine

¼ cup fresh rose petals, never sprayed with pesticides

PREP

Place an 8-by-12-inch glass or metal baking pan in the freezer to chill. The pan should rest flat on an easily accessible spot.

MAKE THE BASE

In a large bowl, combine the water, sugar, and salt, stirring until the sugar and salt are dissolved. Stir in the rose syrup (if using). Stir in the Champagne.

FREEZE

Remove the chilled baking pan from the freezer and pour in the liquid. Return the pan to the freezer. After 30 minutes, use a fork to stir the granita from the outside in, stirring any ice crystals back into the liquid.

ADD THE ROSE PETALS

Using a sharp knife, mince the rose petals. Stir the rose "confetti" into the ice, which should just be starting to form crystals.

Return the pan to the freezer. Stir the granita with a fork every 30 minutes for at least 3 hours, or until the entire mixture has frozen and has a uniformly light, "dry," crystalline texture. When the granita has reached this stage, cover it tightly with plastic wrap until you are ready to serve.

Rose syrup is available in Indian grocery stores or online grocery retailers. It is very concentrated, so a little goes a long, long way.

and to top it off ...

Make your perfectly simple ice cream more perfect by keeping a variety of toppings, sides, or accompaniments on hand. While some of these recipes come together quickly, like Perfectly Whipped Cream (page 207), others take a bit of planning and preparation, such as Chocolate Wafer Cookies (page 217). Ultimately, your guests will be bowled over at the range of mouthwatering toppings, elevating your social from ordinary to unforgettable.

BUTTERSCOTCH
SAUCE

MAKES 1¼ CUPS * PREP TIME: 5 MINUTES * COOK TIME: 10 MINUTES

The difference between butterscotch candy and sauce is only a matter of how long the syrup is cooked. Butterscotch candies were a childhood favorite, so garnishing homemade ice cream with this sauce triggers fond memories. It complements so many flavors, from vanilla to coffee to walnut to pineapple. This sauce comes together in mere minutes, making it a perfect topping choice.

4 tablespoons unsalted butter

1 cup light brown sugar

10 tablespoons heavy (whipping) cream, divided

½ teaspoon pure vanilla extract

In a small, heavy-bottomed saucepan over medium-high heat, combine the butter, sugar, and 5 tablespoons of heavy cream. Bring the mixture to a boil and cook for 3 minutes.

Remove the pan from the heat. When the mixture stops boiling, carefully whisk in the remaining 5 tablespoons of cream. Stir in the vanilla.

Store the sauce in an airtight container in the refrigerator for up to 2 weeks.

CREAMY CARAMEL
SAUCE

MAKES 1 CUP * PREP TIME: 10 MINUTES * COOK TIME: 5 MINUTES

Surely one of our favorites, rich cream combines with sweet butter to accent the edginess of this dark caramel sauce. A balance of sweet and bitter notes derived from the caramelized sugar makes this an essential sauce for your dessert repertoire. It can be swirled into freshly churned ice cream, used as a festive topping for sundaes, and drizzled as an all-purpose dessert sauce for composed confections like a Neapolitan Bombe (page 110). Vary the depth of bitterness according to your tastes by adjusting the caramelization time of the sugar. The lighter the color, the sweeter the finished product will be. The darker the color, the edgier and more bitter it will be.

¾ cup sugar

3 tablespoons water

½ cup heavy (whipping) cream

1 tablespoon unsalted butter

Generous pinch kosher salt

In a small, heavy-bottomed saucepan over medium heat, combine the sugar and water. Cook until the sugar begins to simmer and darken, about 5 minutes. If the sugar begins to caramelize unevenly, gently swirl the pan to achieve an equal color and return to the heat. Do not stir it with a spoon.

When the sugar is a uniformly deep mahogany, turn off the heat and, using a long-handled wooden spoon or heat-proof spatula, slowly incorporate the heavy cream and stir until the mixture is smooth. Take caution as the mixture steams and bubbles violently for a few moments with the first additions of cream. Stir in the butter and salt.

Store in an airtight container in the refrigerator for up to 2 weeks. Bring the sauce to room temperature before using.

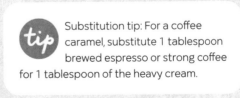

Substitution tip: For a coffee caramel, substitute 1 tablespoon brewed espresso or strong coffee for 1 tablespoon of the heavy cream.

HOT FUDGE
SAUCE

MAKES 2 CUPS * PREP TIME: 10 MINUTES * COOK TIME: 10 MINUTES

Simply put, we believe a sundae is not a sundae without hot fudge sauce drizzled about. The first hot fudge sauce was likely the result of a happy accident in which a fudge recipe did not set properly. Rather than toss the entire sticky potful, the ingenious cook used the concoction as a sauce, and the rest is delicious history. Hot fudge sauce is so simple to make, you'll forgo the jarred stuff for this homemade version every time.

⅔ cup heavy (whipping) cream

½ cup corn syrup

¼ cup unsweetened cocoa powder

2 tablespoons unsalted butter, cut into small cubes

6 ounces bittersweet chocolate, finely chopped

Pinch kosher salt

⅛ teaspoon pure vanilla extract

In a small, heavy-bottomed saucepan over medium-high heat, combine the cream, corn syrup, and cocoa powder. Bring the mixture to a boil, then reduce the heat and simmer gently for 5 minutes. Whisk in the butter until it is melted and fully incorporated.

Place the chocolate in a small heat-proof bowl. Pour the hot mixture over the chocolate. Cover the bowl with plastic wrap and let it sit for 2 minutes. Remove the plastic and gently whisk the mixture until the chocolate is melted and the fudge is smooth and shiny. Stir in the salt and vanilla.

Store in an airtight container in the refrigerator for up to a week (if it lasts that long).

CANDIED NUTS

MAKES 4 CUPS ∗ PREP TIME: 20 MINUTES ∗ COOK TIME: 15 MINUTES

This confection will make you swoon—you will want to eat them out of hand for an anytime snack! A variety of nuts work well here, so select what you prefer or what your budget allows. From coconut shavings to hazelnuts, pistachios to peanuts, these candied nuts increase the fun with every crunchy bite.

1½ cups sugar

1 cup water

½ cup honey

1 teaspoon kosher salt

4 cups nuts, such as almonds, hazelnuts, pistachios, or peanuts, and/or coconut shavings (or a combination)

tip Natural humidity is the enemy of these candied nuts, so storing them in an airtight container or in the freezer is a must. If they become a bit sticky, simply pop them in the freezer for 10 minutes and their crunchy nature returns.

Preheat the oven to 325°F. Line a rimmed baking sheet with parchment paper.

In a heavy-bottomed 4-quart saucepan over high heat, combine the sugar, water, honey, and salt. Bring the liquid to a boil and add the nuts, stirring to evenly coat them. Bring the mixture back to a boil and boil the nuts for 1 minute.

Drain the nuts in a strainer, draining off as much of the syrup from the nuts as possible.

Spread out the nuts in a single layer on the baking sheet. Toast them in the oven, tossing them occasionally to prevent them from burning, about 15 minutes. Let one nut cool on the countertop for a few minutes and test it. It should be golden and snappy. If it is, remove the rest of the nuts from the oven.

Let the candied nuts cool completely before storing them in an airtight container. When ready to use, break them into bite-size pieces or chop finely.

ALL-AMERICAN PEANUT BRITTLE

MAKES ABOUT 14 OUNCES ✳ PREP TIME: 5 MINUTES ✳ COOK TIME: 20 MINUTES

Peanut brittle may be a winter holiday favorite, but as far as we're concerned it should be enjoyed year round. It has flavorful elements everyone loves: a salty crunch pairs with a sweet finish. No wonder it's a perfect ice cream garnish. Peanut brittle's origins are cloudy, but our favorite origin story is that of Paul Bunyan's cousin, Tony Beaver. In an attempt to stop encroaching floodwaters, Tony poured peanuts and molasses into the river. The day was saved and a delicious treat was born. Be brave! Try substituting other nuts in this simple recipe.

½ cup corn syrup

½ cup sugar

2 tablespoons water

1½ cups raw, skinless, unsalted peanuts

Pinch salt

½ teaspoon baking soda

Line a rimmed baking sheet with a silicone baking mat or parchment paper.

In a small, heavy-bottomed pot, combine the corn syrup, sugar, and water over high heat. Bring the mixture to a boil, stirring constantly with a long-handled wooden or heat-proof spoon.

Stir in the peanuts and salt. Clip a candy thermometer to the side of the pot, making sure it is immersed in the liquid but not touching the bottom of the pot. Bring the mixture to a medium boil, stirring occasionally, until the thermometer reads 300°F. The mixture should be a deep golden brown; if it is not, continue cooking for another minute or so or until the color is achieved.

Remove the pot from the heat and take out the thermometer. Immediately add the baking soda and stir until the mixture foams. >>

Quickly and carefully pour the mixture onto the baking sheet. Using a small offset spatula, evenly spread the brittle to a uniform thickness. Resist overworking the candy, as this will deflate the brittle and cause it to lose its attractive honeycomb texture. Do not be concerned if there are clumps; it will break into manageable pieces just the same. Set the baking sheet aside so the brittle can cool completely.

Break the cooled brittle into bite-size pieces and store in an airtight container. It will last for weeks.

 A silicone baking mat (we prefer the Silpat brand) is an indispensable tool for the modern baker. Virtually indestructible, it makes quick work of sticky jobs and can go directly from the freezer to the oven. Cleanup is as easy as soap and water, or it can go in the dishwasher. Invest in a few and you will be baking like a pro in no time.

PERFECTLY WHIPPED CREAM

MAKES 3 CUPS * PREP TIME: 10 MINUTES

Many years ago, Marion Cunningham, the celebrated American food writer, enlightened us regarding the importance of perfectly whipped cream. That conversation triggered a deep appreciation for even the simplest garnishes. Perfectly whipped cream can be a revelation. Slightly sweetened and flavored with a touch of vanilla extract or whole bean, it adds lightness and distinction to almost any frozen dessert.

2 cups heavy (whipping) cream, very cold

1 teaspoon pure vanilla extract or
    1 vanilla bean, split lengthwise
    and seeds scraped out

2 tablespoons sugar

In a large chilled bowl, mix together the cream and vanilla extract or vanilla seeds. Rapidly and steadily whisk the cream by hand until it begins to form soft peaks and the volume increases. Add the sugar and return to whisking. Do not overwhip the cream. The texture should be somewhat loose but still hold a shape; it should not be grainy or overly thick.

Store the whipped cream in the refrigerator until ready to use. Use it the same day you make it.

 If the whipped cream is left to rest for an extended period of time, it will gradually separate into two distinct layers, thick and thin. Use a spatula to fold the two back together, then re-whisk to tighten the cream back to soft peaks.

CHOCOLATE
SAUCE

MAKES 1½ CUPS * PREP TIME: 10 MINUTES * COOK TIME: 20 MINUTES

Chocolate sauce, not to be confused with hot fudge sauce, is *the* essential sauce for your ice cream. Ours is a delightful blend of cocoa powder and chocolate. Store it in the refrigerator until ready to use, then warm it slightly for a pourable drizzle of deep chocolate flavor over anything from Madagascar Vanilla Ice Cream (page 34) to Peanut Butter Ice Cream (page 134), or even blended into a thick Milkshake (page 117).

In a heavy-bottomed 2-quart pot over high heat, bring the water, corn syrup, and sugar to a boil.

Reduce the heat to low and whisk in the cocoa powder. Increase the heat to high again and bring the mixture back to a boil, whisking it occasionally. Just as the mixture boils, remove the pot from the heat and whisk in the chopped chocolate, stirring until it is melted.

Strain the sauce through a fine-mesh strainer and use it immediately or refrigerate in an airtight container until ready to use.

1 cup water

¼ cup corn syrup

½ cup sugar

¾ cup unsweetened cocoa powder, sifted

2 ounces bittersweet chocolate, finely chopped

STRAWBERRY
SAUCE

MAKES 2 CUPS * PREP TIME: 5 MINUTES

This versatile sauce pairs well with many different flavors. It naturally complements Strawberry Ice Cream (page 36), is one of the stars of the Banana Split (page 119), and pairs with Lemon Ice Cream (page 100) for a sweet-sour delight. It is up to you how chunky or smooth you prefer the finished sauce or if you would rather strain the seeds out entirely. This sauce relies on well-ripened, juicy strawberries and is never better than at the height of the berry season.

3 pints strawberries

2 tablespoons sugar, or more to taste

Generous pinch kosher salt

Kirschwasser (optional)

Hull the strawberries and cut them into quarters. Place them in a food processor and purée them to your preferred consistency, chunky or fully smooth.

For a smooth strawberry sauce, strain the purée through a medium-mesh strainer.

Stir in the sugar, salt, and Kirschwasser (if using). Taste the sauce and adjust, adding more sugar or Kirschwasser if needed.

Refrigerate in an airtight container until ready to use.

 This sauce freezes very well, so make extra when the berries are abundant, flavorful, and cheap and then defrost as needed throughout the year.

WARM CARAMELIZED PINEAPPLE
WITH RUM

MAKES ABOUT 6 CUPS * PREP TIME: 20 MINUTES * COOK TIME: 30 MINUTES

This pineapple topping is robust and flavorful with a wonderful texture. It certainly beats the topping we remember from our childhood ice cream shop. In fact, we ended up eating this right out of the pan before we even got out the ice cream! But be patient, it is even better over ice cream.

1 ripe pineapple

4 tablespoons unsalted butter, divided

6 tablespoons sugar, divided

4 tablespoons rum, divided

½ teaspoon pure vanilla extract, divided

With a sharp knife, cut off the top and bottom of the pineapple. Remove the outer surface by cutting it off in strips, starting at the top and slicing downward with the curve of the pineapple. Don't cut too deeply. Next, using the tip of a potato peeler or knife, remove the eyes. Cut the pineapple in quarters and remove the core piece from each. Cut each quarter lengthwise into three long pieces and slice each of these into about ten ½-inch chunks. Divide the pineapple chunks between two medium bowls.

Heat a large cast iron pan over medium-high heat and add 2 tablespoons of butter. When the butter is melted, add one bowl of pineapple chunks. Sauté the pineapple for 3 to 4 minutes. The fruit will let off a lot of juice during this phase of the cooking. When you begin to see a little color on the fruit, add 3 tablespoons of sugar to the pan and continue to cook the pineapple. The pineapple will take on more color and the juice will begin to reduce and caramelize. Shake and stir the pan occasionally to make sure the fruit is browning evenly.

When the liquid becomes syrupy and caramelized and the pineapple is nicely browned, typically after 8 to 10 minutes, turn off the heat and stir in 2 tablespoons of rum and $\frac{1}{4}$ teaspoon of vanilla. Transfer the pineapple to a bowl and repeat this step for the second batch of pineapple, using the remaining ingredients.

The finished pineapple should be used the day it is made, preferably within a few hours. As it sits, the caramel seeps into the fruit and it no longer retains its lovely yellow color. Serve slightly warm or at room temperature.

CHOCOLATE-COVERED NUTS

MAKES 14 OUNCES ✳ PREP TIME: 10 MINUTES ✳ COOK TIME: 15 MINUTES

This is the perfect fold-in for many flavors of ice cream, or simply as a sprinkle on top—if you can keep yourself from eating them all before your ice cream is made. There is a great solution to this problem: Just make extra.

3 ounces nuts, such as almonds, pecans, or walnuts (or a combination), roughly chopped

4 ounces semisweet or bittersweet chocolate

tip You can use any combinations of nuts you'd like, or be a purist and use only one kind. For an added chewy texture, add 1 to 2 tablespoons dried currants or dried cherries to the chocolate with the nuts.

Preheat the oven to 350°F.

Line two baking sheets with parchment paper and place the nuts in a single layer on one of the baking sheets. Toast the nuts until lightly brown, stirring occasionally, 12 to 14 minutes.

In a double boiler or a stainless-steel bowl set over a pot of barely simmering water, melt the chocolate, stirring it with a heat-proof spatula. Remove the bowl from the heat.

While the nuts are still warm, add them to the melted chocolate and stir until they are completely coated. Pour the mixture onto the second baking sheet and spread out the nuts with the back of the spatula. Allow the mixture to cool completely, then cover the baking sheet with plastic wrap and refrigerate.

When the nuts are cold, transfer them to a cutting board and roughly chop. Store the chopped nuts in an airtight container in the refrigerator until ready to use.

CANDIED GRAPEFRUIT SLICES

MAKES ABOUT 20 SLICES * PREP TIME: 20 MINUTES * COOK TIME: 1 HOUR, 15 MINUTES

This method of candying slices of citrus is simple and makes this a very versatile ingredient to have handy. This recipe works not only with grapefruit, but with lemons, oranges, and tangerines as well. The key is slow cooking.

1½ cups sugar

¾ cup water

1 small pink grapefruit

Combine the sugar and water in a saucepan and bring to a boil over medium-high heat, stirring to dissolve the sugar. Remove the pan from the heat.

Using a very sharp knife, cut the grapefruit in half through the stem end. Lay the grapefruit halves cut-side down on a cutting board. Slice off the stem and bottom ends of the grapefruit. Cut the grapefruit into very thin slices, as thin as you can make them, removing any seeds as you come across them.

Layer the slices in a 10-inch sauté pan, overlapping them slightly if needed so they all fit in the pan. Pour the warm sugar syrup over the fruit. Cover the slices with a piece of parchment paper and then cover the whole pan with aluminum foil. Place the pan over low heat and gently cook the slices for 30 minutes. Turn off the heat and let the covered pan sit for another 30 minutes. Remove the foil and parchment paper and put the heat on low. Finish cooking the fruit, barely at a simmer, for about 8 minutes. Remove the pan from the heat and let the grapefruit slices cool completely.

The fruit slices should be a lovely transparent pink, soft and flexible. Pack the cooled candied fruit slices and remaining syrup in a jar with a tight-fitting lid. They will keep indefinitely if covered in syrup and kept in the refrigerator.

WAFFLE CONE

MAKES 10 TO 12 CONES ✳ PREP TIME: 15 MINUTES ✳ COOK TIME: 30 MINUTES

Everyone loves a crunchy-sweet waffle cone filled with scoops of their favorite ice cream. We've developed a gluten-free waffle cone that comes together quickly and easily. Invest in a small, relatively inexpensive waffle maker and turn out crisp homemade waffle cones in no time at all.

4 tablespoons unsalted butter

2 extra-large eggs

½ cup sugar

3 tablespoons whole milk

¼ teaspoon pure vanilla extract

⅛ teaspoon kosher salt

½ cup Bob's Red Mill Gluten-Free
    1-to-1 Baking Flour

 tip Bob's Red Mill Gluten-Free 1-to-1 Baking Flour is available in stores such as Whole Foods Markets or from online retailers like Amazon.com.

Preheat the waffle iron to medium.

In a small saucepan or in the microwave, melt the butter. Allow it to cool, but still be pourable.

In the bowl of a standing electric mixer, whisk the eggs and sugar on high speed until they are foamy and hold a peak.

Stir the milk into the cooled butter. With the mixer on low speed, add the butter and milk mixture to the bowl and mix until fully incorporated. Add the vanilla and mix until fully incorporated.

Mix the salt into the flour. Add half of it to the bowl and mix until combined. Add the remaining flour and salt and mix until combined. The batter should be slightly thick but pourable.

Place 2 tablespoons of batter in the center of the waffle iron and close the lid. When the waffle is a deep golden brown, remove it and immediately shape it into a cone. The first cone will tell you if you want a thicker batter (stir another teaspoon or two of flour into the batter to achieve this) or a thicker cone (add a little more batter to the cone maker).

Use the same day if possible to ensure a crisp waffle cone.

ROASTED CHERRIES

MAKES 2½ CUPS ✳ PREP TIME: 5 MINUTES ✳ COOK TIME: 20 TO 30 MINUTES

We look forward to cherry season each year with great anticipation. In mid-spring Bing, Brooks, and Queen Anne varietals start to flood the California farmers' markets. We process as many as we can and hoard them for use in Cherry Ice Pops (page 116) and these simply roasted cherries for topping sundaes.

1 pound cherries, such as Bing, pitted

¼ cup sugar

2 teaspoons water

1 tablespoon Kirschwasser (optional)

Preheat the oven to 400°F.

In a large bowl, toss the cherries with the sugar, water, and Kirschwasser (if using). Place the cherries and any liquid in a baking pan large enough to hold the cherries in a single layer.

Roast the cherries, stirring once or twice, until the fruit becomes concentrated and juicy, 20 to 30 minutes. If they appear to be drying out, stir in a sprinkling of water to moisten. When the fruit is tender and the juices have reduced, remove the pan from the oven and completely cool the cherries. Store the cherries in a small container with a tight-fitting lid and refrigerate until ready to use.

CHOCOLATE WAFER COOKIES

MAKES 24 TO 28 COOKIES * PREP TIME: 30 MINUTES, PLUS CHILLING
COOK TIME: 12 TO 15 MINUTES

Whether sandwiched around or crumbled into your favorite ice cream or on their own, these cookies are just what the doctor ordered. You can bake them a little on the soft side—perfect for ice cream sandwiches—or crispy enough to be crumbled as a topping. The addition of finely chopped chocolate adds a little extra punch.

¾ cup (1½ sticks) unsalted butter,
    at room temperature

1¼ cups sugar

1 extra-large egg

½ teaspoon pure vanilla extract

1½ cups all-purpose flour, plus
    more for dusting

¾ cup unsweetened cocoa powder

½ teaspoon baking powder

⅛ teaspoon kosher salt

2 tablespoons finely chopped bittersweet
    or semisweet chocolate

In a standing mixer fitted with the paddle attachment, cream the butter and sugar until smooth. Add the egg and vanilla and mix thoroughly.

In a medium-size bowl, combine the flour, cocoa, baking powder, and salt. Use a whisk to gently combine the dry ingredients so that they become uniform in color. Add one-third of the dry ingredients to the butter mixture and mix. Once incorporated, stop the machine, scrape down the sides of the bowl, and add half of the remaining dry ingredients. Again, once incorporated, stop the machine and scrape down the sides of the bowl before adding and mixing in the last of the flour. Add the chopped chocolate to the bowl. Mix to incorporate completely.

Turn out the dough onto a lightly floured board and roll it into a log measuring about $7\frac{1}{2}$ inches long and $2\frac{1}{2}$ inches in diameter. Wrap the log tightly in plastic wrap and chill the dough thoroughly in the refrigerator. >>

Preheat the oven to 350°F. Line a baking sheet pan with parchment paper or a silicone baking mat.

Evenly slice the chilled dough log into 12 to 14 cookies. Arrange them on the baking sheet with a little room in between each cookie to allow for even baking and for spread.

Bake the cookies for 12 to 15 minutes, depending on whether you want them chewy or crispy. Let the finished cookies cool completely before using or storing.

tip To make a vanilla and chocolate swirl cookie, divide the butter and egg mixture between two bowls. To one bowl, mix in 6 tablespoons unsweetened cocoa powder, ¾ cup flour, ¼ teaspoon baking powder, 1 tablespoon chopped chocolate, and a generous pinch of kosher salt; to the second bowl mix in 1¼ cups flour, ¼ teaspoon baking powder, and a generous pinch of kosher salt. Now you have chocolate dough and vanilla dough. Divide each into two or three balls, combine them alternately, and roll into a log. Twist the log a bit or fold it once to get a nice swirl pattern, but don't overwork it or it will end up muddy. This makes a festive-looking cookie; each one will be unique.

CANDIED FRUIT CHIPS

Elevate any frozen treat with these elegant candied fruit garnishes. When ripe fruit is thinly sliced, slowly poached in a deeply flavorful sugar syrup, and then oven-dried, it creates concentrated, flavorful fruit chips. Just about any fruit can be candied this way. We use Pink Lady apples here, but Bosc pears work the same way, and we also provide tips for candying pineapple (see the Tip). Likewise, the sugar syrup can be flavored with a host of warm spice combinations like star anise, cloves, and black pepper, or with citrus zest, vanilla beans, or aged rum.

1 Pink Lady apple or Bosc pear

1½ cups sugar

1½ cups water

½ Madagascar vanilla bean and/or 2 star anise pods and/or 3 whole cloves (optional)

2 tablespoons aged rum (optional)

Slice the apple or pear $\frac{1}{16}$ inch thick on a mandoline. Discard the seeds.

In a small, heavy-bottomed pot over medium-low heat, bring the sugar, water, vanilla (if using), and rum (if using) to a simmer. Place the fruit slices in the syrup. Cut out a round piece of parchment paper and place it on top of the fruit to keep it submerged in the syrup. Simmer the fruit slices until translucent, about 25 minutes.

Meanwhile, preheat the oven to 200°F. Line a baking sheet with parchment paper or a silicone baking mat.

Carefully transfer the poached fruit slices from the syrup to a clean kitchen towel and pat the slices dry. Place the slices in a single layer on the baking sheet and dry them in the oven for 2 to $2\frac{1}{2}$ hours.

Allow the candied fruit slices to cool for 10 minutes before storing them in an airtight container.

 For candied pineapple, peel, core, and remove any eyes from the pineapple. Slice the pineapple into ¼-inch-thick slices. Follow the steps for poaching in the sugar syrup, but add an extra 1 tablespoon of rum (if using) to the sugar syrup.

ACKNOWLEDGMENTS

FROM ANTHONY:

Lindsey Shere, who has been an inspiration, a guiding light, a teacher, and most of all a friend these many years. Lindsey, you profoundly influenced my sensibilities and tastes, challenged me to be a better chef, and taught me to think critically about what I eat. Your unique style continues to influence professional and home cooks alike. Thank you for sharing your vision with us.

The farmers and fruit growers of California that bestow upon us arguably the world's most perfect produce. Without this network of hard working people we would be adrift in a sea of mediocre food.

Art Pollard at Amano Chocolate Company for his kind words and sensational products.

Thanks to Alice Waters and the staff of Chez Panisse Restaurant and Café for providing a truly unique work environment where co-workers become family and the vision of informed eating remains paramount.

Hannah Love for your time and energy with communication and coordination.

Jessica Leng for your creative input, time, and expert dessert knowledge.

Thanks to Sara Remington Photography and Studio 1568 in Emeryville, California for providing an ideal space to create and capture the perfect scoop.

Photographer Kelly Ishikawa and stylist Rod Hipskind for once again making the ordinary seem extraordinary.

Our editor at Callisto Media, Talia Platz, for keeping our project on the right track and encouraging our vision.

Callisto Media's Senior Art Director Katy Brown for her leadership and expertise on making a truly special ice cream book.

Mary Jo Baca for providing us with her unique collection of "aged" glassware.

And finally, sincere thanks to Frances Baca, who worked tirelessly on the design and implementation of our blurry vision, from taste testing ice cream to guiding the most minute artistic nuance.

FROM MARY JO:

I would like to thank Lindsey Shere first and foremost for welcoming me into her pastry kitchen at Chez Panisse in 1981. I'm not sure why she actually did that since I had never worked in a professional kitchen before and I could offer little more than my enthusiasm and Midwestern work ethic.

Her skill, patience, and good humor made my learning experience fruitful, happy, and memorable. For this I am very grateful.

I would also like to thank Alice Waters for giving me a shot at it too. I cannot say enough how profoundly being at her little Berkeley restaurant changed everything. Her relentless drive to find the best products and the best people, and to educate us—and indeed the world—about the importance of healthful eating and being responsible stewards of our generous planet has had a tremendous impact. No detail is too small when it comes to her vision. I am happy to be a part of it.

Thank you to Pastry Chef Carrie Lewis, one of the hardest working, most talented, and earnest people I know. I am a better cook for working side-by-side with you these past five years. You are a gem.

To the pastry team at Chez Panisse: Patricia Salvati, McKenzie Funk, Cassie Johns, Eriko Yahiro, and a special thanks to Jessica Leng, who jumped in to assist with the styling of the photographs with her ever-cheery and enthusiastic energy. It is a pleasure to work with you all, to see you grow, and to share ideas.

To Curt, my rock, for your support, integrity, and seemingly endless energy. Thank you for your honest opinions and your dedication to tasting the never ending bowls of ice cream put in front of you.

To all the talented and tireless people at Callisto Media: Katy Brown, Frances Baca, and Talia Platz, whose "never-a-problem-only-a-solution" attitude was invaluable. Thank you for helping to make this a fun and educational project. Thanks to photographer Kelly Ishikawa and stylist Rod Hopskind for creating the beautiful photographs before everything melted!

ABOUT THE AUTHORS

ANTHONY TASSINELLO has spent the last two decades cooking at Alice Waters' Chez Panisse restaurant in Berkeley, California. His passion for baking, pastry, cocktail culture, and wood-fired cookery keeps him busy all four seasons. He has foraged for wild mushrooms from Oregon to Italy, and was Michael Pollan's foraging guide in his acclaimed bestseller, *The Omnivore's Dilemma*. He is the author of *The Essential Wood-Fired Pizza Cookbook*, and his work has appeared in *The New York Times Magazine*, *San Francisco Magazine*, The Huffington Post, and on NPR. He lives in Northern California with his girlfriend Frances, her son Bruno, and their orange cat, Rooney.

MARY JO THORESEN is pastry chef at Alice Waters' Chez Panisse restaurant, where she began her career as an intern in 1981. She worked side-by-side founding pastry chef Lindsey Shere for twelve years before opening Amici Café at the California College of Arts with her husband Curt Clingman. In 1999 they opened their beloved bistro Jojo in Oakland, California, and ran it for nearly a decade. Mary Jo has been back at Chez Panisse since 2008. Her work has appeared in *San Francisco Magazine*, *Bon Appètit*, *Gourmet*, *Oprah Magazine*, the *San Francisco Chronicle*, and *Oakland Magazine*. She lives in Northern California with her husband Curt and their very entertaining cat Mickey.

REFERENCES

Del Conte, Anna. *Gastronomy of Italy*. London: Pavilion Books, 2013.

Goldstein, Darra, editor. *The Oxford Companion to Sugar and Sweets*. New York: Oxford University Press, 2015.

Lebovitz, David. *The Perfect Scoop*. Berkeley: Ten Speed Press, 2010.

May, Tony. *Italian Cuisine: Basic Cooking Techniques*. Bologna: Italian Food and Wine Institute, 1990.

Shere, Lindsey. *Chez Panisse Desserts*. New York: Random House, 1994.

Waters, Alice. *Chez Panisse Fruit*. New York: William Morrow, 2002

MEASUREMENT CONVERSION CHARTS

VOLUME EQUIVALENTS (LIQUID)

US STANDARD	US STANDARD (OUNCES)	METRIC (APPROXIMATE)
2 tablespoons	1 fl. oz.	30 mL
¼ cup	2 fl. oz.	60 mL
½ cup	4 fl. oz.	120 mL
1 cup	8 fl. oz.	240 mL
1½ cups	12 fl. oz.	355 mL
2 cups or 1 pint	16 fl. oz.	475 mL
4 cups or 1 quart	32 fl. oz.	1 L
1 gallon	128 fl. oz.	4 L

OVEN TEMPERATURES

FAHRENHEIT (F)	CELSIUS (C) (APPROXIMATE)
250°F	120°C
300°F	150°C
325°F	165°C
350°F	180°C
375°F	190°C
400°F	200°C
425°F	220°C
450°F	230°C

VOLUME EQUIVALENTS (DRY)

US STANDARD	METRIC (APPROXIMATE)
⅛ teaspoon	0.5 mL
¼ teaspoon	1 mL
½ teaspoon	2 mL
¾ teaspoon	4 mL
1 teaspoon	5 mL
1 tablespoon	15 mL
¼ cup	59 mL
⅓ cup	79 mL
½ cup	118 mL
⅔ cup	156 mL
¾ cup	177 mL
1 cup	235 mL
2 cups or 1 pint	475 mL
3 cups	700 mL
4 cups or 1 quart	1 L

WEIGHT EQUIVALENTS

US STANDARD	METRIC (APPROXIMATE)
½ ounce	15 g
1 ounce	30 g
2 ounces	60 g
4 ounces	115 g
8 ounces	225 g
12 ounces	340 g
16 ounces or 1 pound	455 g

RECIPE INDEX

INDEX

notes

NOTES

NOTES

NOTES

NOTES

NOTES